THE CIVIL WAR *Sewing Circle*

Quilts and Sewing Accessories Inspired by the Era

KATHLEEN TRACY

Martingale®
& COMPANY

The Civil War Sewing Circle:
Quilts and Sewing Accessories Inspired by the Era
© 2011 by Kathleen Tracy

That Patchwork Place® is an imprint
of Martingale & Company®.

Martingale & Company
19021 120th Ave. NE, Suite 102
Bothell, WA 98011-9511 USA
www.martingale-pub.com

Printed in China
16 15 14 13 12 11   8 7 6 5 4 3 2 1

Library of Congress Cataloging-in-Publication Data is available upon request.

ISBN: 978-1-60468-005-8

MISSION STATEMENT

*Dedicated to providing quality products
and service to inspire creativity.*

CREDITS

President & CEO: Tom Wierzbicki
Editor in Chief: Mary V. Green
Managing Editor: Tina Cook
Developmental Editor: Karen Costello Soltys
Technical Editor: Ellen Pahl
Copy Editor: Sheila Chapman Ryan
Design Director: Stan Green
Production Manager: Regina Girard
Illustrator: Laurel Strand
Cover & Text Designer: Regina Girard
Photographer: Brent Kane

PHOTO AND QUOTATION CREDITS

Diary entries and letters on pages 9, 21–23, 33, 34, and 47–49 are reprinted with permission from *The American Civil War: Letters and Diaries,* online database published by Alexander Street Press, Alexandria, VA: 2001.

Photo of little girls sewing on cover and title page are from Ellen Taylor, family collection. Photos on pages 5, 9, 10, 22, 23, 34, 48, and 49 are from the Library of Congress. Photos on pages 3, 4, 34, 35, 63, 72, and 78 are from the author's personal collection.

Dedication

To Paul, for his patience, love and support

Acknowledgments

I sincerely wish to thank all of the people at Martingale & Company who have worked so hard to make this book even better than I imagined.

Thank you to Ellen Pahl and Sheila Ryan for their editorial expertise.

Thanks to Eileen Lawrence of Alexander Street Publishing for permission to use the online database *The American Civil War: Letters and Diaries* as my source for the letters and diaries.

Special thanks to Jill Meszaros for helping me out and piecing the blocks for "Union Stars Quilt" on page 11.

I'd like to thank Dawn Larsen for machine quilting "Union Stars Quilt" on page 11, "Double Hourglass Quilt" on page 15, "Soldier's Cot Quilt" on page 29, and "Album Quilt" on page 64.

Many thanks to Katie Reed for making the wool felt appliqué for "Wool Appliqué Sewing Box" on page 67.

I'm grateful to Lynn Rice and Gail Smith for their zero-hour help with the bindings on some of the quilts.

Many thanks to the Fairfield Processing Corporation for their 100% natural cotton batting that was used to give the quilts an antique look.

A special thank you to all of the women in my Yahoo! online quilting group, SmallQuiltTalk, who made the blocks that became the wonderful "Friendship Album Quilt" on page 39. Thanks so much to Bonnie Stapleton for generously giving her time and energy to quilt the quilt.

Thanks again to my family and friends for their continued support of and pride in my creative pursuits. Paul, your wisdom and advice help me more than you know. Thank you, Caitlin, for your keen eye that often helped me choose just the right fabric for my borders or the right setting for the blocks. I think it's in your genes! Thanks, Evan, for being patient with me and reminding me to "calm down" and also for making me laugh when I needed to.

Lastly, I am extremely grateful to all the fans of my books who inspire me with their dedication and joy in making simple quilts.

CONTENTS

INTRODUCTION

"If all that has been said by orators and poets since the creation of the world in praise of women were applied to the women of America, it would not do them justice for their conduct during this war. God Bless the women of America!"

~*Abraham Lincoln, from* The Collected Works of Abraham Lincoln

If the Civil War was a turning point in American history, then it could also be said that it was a turning point in women's history as well. When the first shots of the war were fired in the spring of 1861 and President Lincoln called for volunteers, both men and women responded with action: men by enlisting in droves and women by establishing aid societies. Local aid societies sprang up in towns and cities across the nation. Groups like the U.S. Christian Commission, the U.S. Sanitary Commission, and other soldiers' aid societies distributed thousands of blankets and quilts, as well as food, clothing, and medical supplies to the troops. Countless numbers of women organized their church groups and sewing circles to do what they could to support the enlisted men. In the early days of the war, the sewing circles were informal; as the need for quilts and bedding grew, they became more organized. It's estimated that over 250,000 quilts were eventually sewn by these local sewing circles and donated to the U.S. Sanitary Commission during a time when they were so desperately needed.

During the course of writing an earlier book, *Remembering Adelia,* I was struck by the strong sense of community conveyed in Adelia's diary, particularly as the nation went to war in 1861. I became eager to learn more about the sisterhood of quilting during this time period and curious about the ways in which women bonded together for support and used their sewing skills for community service. Women's experiences during the war were varied and most women were not only affected by it but also transformed in some way. Their lives inside and outside the home changed after the war. It's likely that community-service activities like the sewing circles and subsequent fundraisers were especially useful in helping women gain skills that advanced their organizational and leadership abilities, leading to political involvement, further work in paid positions, and enumerable opportunities later in the century.

It's interesting to see the events we only read about in history books unfold on the pages of simple letters written to loved ones. I've chosen to introduce the chapters with excerpts from some of these letters, and one of the most difficult things about writing this book was deciding which excerpts to include. Originally, I did not intend to include any diary entries or personal accounts from the time. However, when I stumbled upon the letters and a few diary passages

expressing the thoughts and sentiments of women and men of the period, I knew I had to include some of them, particularly the now-famous letter written by Sullivan Ballou to his wife a week before he was killed (page 10). Many letters that I read were extremely personal and full of emotion; they contained much more private content than diaries of the era. These letter excerpts introducing the chapters embody in a very personal way many of the thoughts and emotions of those who lived and fought during this time and give us a much better sense of what people were experiencing than any history book ever could. The world as they knew it was changed by the war; their lives were dramatically changed after the war and in the years that followed. The letters and quotes also give us wonderful insight into how those who lived through this turbulent time perceived the world and also how women's sewing in particular impacted the war and eventually changed women's place in society.

The quilts included in this book were inspired by some of the simple patterns and fabrics that were popular during the nineteenth century and represent the tremendous effort made by ordinary women as they pulled together and influenced the path of history. I have included a number of patterns for small doll quilts as well, not only because they're fun and easy to make, but also to engage your heart while you're making them. There's something absolutely charming about antique doll quilts and, to me, the imperfect patches and awkward stitches tell a story as acutely as words. So, if you're new to quilting, I suggest that you try one of the smaller projects to help you get started (such as the small quilts on pages 24 and 52). A doll quilt is a great way to try out your skills and learn new ones, in the same way that children of the nineteenth century learned to sew and quilt. See "Quiltmaking Basics" (page 73) for additional help.

Unlike quilters of yesterday, quilters today no longer make their quilts out of necessity. They quilt to feed their spirits and to make lasting items of beauty. There's something wonderfully relaxing about quilting—women knew it then and we haven't forgotten today. As you take your journey through the past, I know that you'll be inspired by the letters and stories that are intertwined with these quilts. I also sincerely hope that you enjoy stitching these simple quilts and projects as much as I have loved making them.

A DREADFUL WAR

A house divided against itself cannot stand.

~Abraham Lincoln's "House Divided" Speech in Springfield, Illinois, June 16, 1858

Richmond, March 4, 1864

My dear Son . . .

Oh how anxious I am to have this dreadful war over, that I might once more see my dear boy back home. I sometimes feel nearly wild but pray continually to God to keep all of mine and me in the right way or I would be a maniac. May God bless and keep you, my dear child, from all harm and guide your steps aright—

Your devoted
Mother

~Letter from Varina Anne Banks Howell Davis to Jefferson Davis Howell

The Civil War was a pivotal point in the history of the United States, ending slavery as well as consolidating the Northern States in a fight to save the Union. As a result of the war, the country was more united than it ever had been before, but not without tremendous cost—it still remains the war with the most casualties in our nation's history. It was a war in which more than 620,000 American men died—many at each other's hands—something that seems almost inconceivable to us today. In the 1862 battle of Fredericksburg alone, Union losses for *the day* were over 12,000 men.

Yet it might very well have been the most important war that America has ever fought. American women watched as their husbands, fathers, and sons went off to battle in 1861, knowing that they might be killed. History books tell us all about the confrontation through military campaigns and strategies but with the exception of the women who served as nurses and spies, the monumental role that ordinary women played is often left out.

Most women were altered drastically by the war in many ways. When the war began, thousands of men enlisted voluntarily. Women took an active role as well and were not as passive as many history books would have us believe by their exclusion. They did more than nurse the sick. Their motives were as diverse as those of the men. Some had a pure and simple desire to serve their country. Others had sons, brothers, husbands, fathers, or lovers in the army, and served in order to be near or to be of some help. Some threw themselves into charitable activities to soothe their grief and pain. For whatever reasons, women's involvement in wartime activities gave them a multitude of experience in public life. And, without their extraordinary efforts on the home front, the outcome of the war may have been very different.

Camp Clark, Washington, D.C.
July the 14th, 1861

My very dear Sarah:

The indications are very strong that we shall move in a few days—perhaps tomorrow. Lest I should not be able to write you again, I feel impelled to write lines that may fall under your eye when I shall be no more.

Our movement may be one of a few days' duration and full of pleasure—and it may be one of severe conflict and death to me. Not my will, but thine O God, be done. If it is necessary that I should fall on the battlefield for my country, I am ready. I have no misgivings about, or lack of confidence in, the cause in which I am engaged, and my courage does not halt or falter. I know how strongly American Civilization now leans upon the triumph of the Government, and how great a debt we owe to those who went before us through the blood and suffering of the Revolution. And I am willing—perfectly willing—to lay down all my joys in this life, to help maintain this Government, and to pay that debt. . . .

I cannot describe to you my feelings on this calm summer night, when two thousand men are sleeping around me, many of them enjoying the last, perhaps, before that of death. . . .

Sarah, my love for you is deathless, it seems to bind me to you with mighty cables that nothing but Omnipotence could break; and yet my love of Country comes over me like a strong wind and bears me irresistibly on with all these chains to the battlefield.

The memories of the blissful moments I have spent with you come creeping over me, and I feel most gratified to God and to you that I have enjoyed them so long. . . . If I do not, my dear Sarah, never forget how much I love you, and when my last breath escapes me on the battlefield, it will whisper your name.

Forgive my many faults, and the many pains I have caused you. How thoughtless and foolish I have oftentimes been! How gladly would I wash out with my tears every little spot upon your happiness, and struggle with all the misfortune of this world, to shield you and my children from harm. But I cannot. I must watch you from the spirit land and hover near you, while you buffet the storms with your precious little freight, and wait with sad patience till we meet to part no more.

But, O Sarah! If the dead can come back to this earth and flit unseen around those they loved, I shall always be near you; in the garish day and in the darkest night—amidst your happiest scenes and gloomiest hours—always, always; and if there be a soft breeze upon your cheek, it shall be my breath; or the cool air fans your throbbing temple, it shall be my spirit passing by.

Sarah, do not mourn me dead; think I am gone and wait for thee, for we shall meet again.

As for my little boys, they will grow as I have done, and never know a father's love and care. Little Willie is too young to remember me long, and my blue-eyed Edgar will keep my frolics with him among the dimmest memories of his childhood. Sarah, I have unlimited confidence in your maternal care and your development of their characters. Tell my two mothers his and hers I call God's blessing upon them. O Sarah, I wait for you there! Come to me, and lead thither my children.

Sullivan

~Letter from Sullivan Ballou to his wife, Sarah, one week before he died.
(Sullivan Ballou letter reprinted from *The Civil War Home Page*, www.civil-war.net.)

Union Stars Quilt

Blocks pieced by Jill Meszaros. Machine quilted by Dawn Larsen.

Finished quilt: 50½" x 64½"

Finished block: 12" x 12"

The Civil War was a pivotal event in American history. Until 1864, America was a republic; after the war it became a nation. Patriotism during this time was high and many women expressed their love for country by volunteering. Ladies aid societies received and forwarded supplies to be distributed to the sick and wounded in camp, field, and general hospitals. Women's work in the war was sometimes a lesson in patience and patriotism as they organized faithfully and ministered to the men who fought to keep the union together.

MATERIALS

Yardage is based on 42"-wide, 100% cotton fabric.

1⅝ yards of red print for outer border

1⅓ yards *total* of assorted shirting prints for block backgrounds

1 fat eighth *each* of 5 different red prints for star points

½ yard of tan print for sashing

1 fat eighth *each* of 4 different medium blue prints for star points

1 fat eighth *each* of 3 different dark blue prints for star points

⅓ yard *total* of 6 different patriotic prints for star centers

⅛ yard of brown print for sashing squares

1 piece, 6" x 6", *each* of 12 assorted red, blue, taupe, and gold prints for blocks

½ yard of a dark blue print for binding

3⅝ yards of fabric for backing

57" x 71" piece of cotton batting

CUTTING

Cutting for 1 Block (Cut 12 total)

From a patriotic print, cut:

• 1 square, 4½" x 4½"

From a shirting print, cut:

• 2 squares, 5¼" x 5¼"; cut into quarters diagonally to make 8 triangles

• 4 squares, 2⅞" x 2⅞"; cut in half diagonally to make 8 triangles

• 4 squares, 2½" x 2½"

From a red, dark blue, *or* medium blue print for star points, cut:

• 2 squares, 5¼" x 5¼"; cut into quarters diagonally to make 8 triangles

From a contrasting red, dark blue, *or* medium blue print, cut:

• 4 squares, 2⅞" x 2⅞"; cut in half diagonally to make 8 triangles

From a red, blue, taupe, or gold scrap, cut:

• 4 squares, 2½" x 2½"

Cutting for Sashing, Borders, and Binding

From the tan print, cut:

• 17 strips, 2½" x 12½"

From the brown print, cut:

• 6 squares, 2½" x 2½"

From the red print for outer border, cut on the *lengthwise grain*:

• 2 strips, 5½ " x 54½"

• 2 strips, 5½" x 50½"

From the dark blue print for binding, cut:

• 6 strips, 2½" x 42"

MAKING THE BLOCKS

The instructions are written for making one block at a time using a variety of red, blue, gold, and light shirting prints. Some fabrics may be used more than once. In my quilt, there are five stars with red points, three stars with dark blue points, and four stars with medium blue points. All of the stars have contrasting secondary points in the background and a patriotic print square in the center. Use the same shirting print throughout each block.

1. Choose eight matching red, dark blue, or medium blue 5¼" triangles for the main star points and eight shirting print 5¼" triangles. Sew a light triangle to a dark triangle. Join pairs of triangles together. Make eight units.

Make 8.

2. Sew two of the units together as shown to make an hourglass unit. Make four.

Make 4.

3. Choose the red or blue 2⅞" triangles for the secondary star points. Sew one triangle to a shirting print 2⅞" triangle. Make eight.

Make 8.

4. Choose red, blue, gold, or taupe print 2½" squares. Sew a square to a unit from step 3. Make four.

Make 4.

5. Sew the remaining units from step 3 to a shirting 2½" square. Make four.

Make 4.

6. Combine the units from step 4 with the units from step 5 as shown. Make four.

Make 4.

7. Arrange the units from step 6, the hourglass units from step 2, and a patriotic print 4½" square into rows as shown. Sew the units into rows. Press. Sew the rows together to make the block.

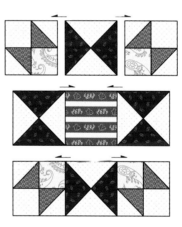

8. Repeat steps 1–7 to make 12 blocks.

Make 12.

ASSEMBLING THE QUILT TOP

1. Sew three blocks together with two tan print 2½" x 12½" sashing strips to make a row. Press the seam allowances toward the sashing. Make four rows.

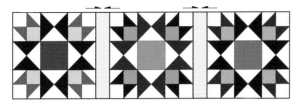

Make 4.

2. Sew three tan print 2½" x 12½" sashing strips together with two brown 2½" squares to make a sashing row. Press the seam allowances toward the sashing strips. Make three rows.

Make 3.

3. Sew the rows of blocks and sashing together, pressing the seam allowances toward the sashing rows.

4. Sew the red print 5½" x 54½" strips to the sides of the quilt. Press toward the border. Sew the 5½" x 50½" strips to the top and bottom of the quilt; press toward the border.

FINISHING THE QUILT

1. Layer the quilt top, batting, and backing; baste the layers together as shown in "Putting the Quilt Together" (page 75). The quilt shown was machine quilted with a feathered-wreath design over the center of the star blocks and a wavy stripe along the borders.

2. Attach the dark blue print binding to the quilt, referring to "Binding" (page 76).

Double Hourglass Quilt

Machine quilted by Dawn Larsen.

Finished quilt: 49" x 49"

Finished block: 6" x 6"

During the Civil War, most women remained on the home front, patiently waiting for word about their husbands, sons, fathers, and other men who had enlisted. Women would gather at train depots to hear casualty lists read aloud. I chose the Double Hourglass block for this quilt as a reminder of how the days, weeks, months, and years may have crept by slowly as women waited to hear news about their loved ones.

MATERIALS

Yardage is based on 42"-wide, 100% cotton fabric.

1½ yards of green print for inner and outer borders

⅞ yard of light green print for alternate blocks and setting triangles

¾ yard *total* of assorted light or shirting prints for block backgrounds

⅓ yard of medium blue print for middle border

Scraps (3" x 6" pieces) of 16 assorted medium and dark prints for blocks

½ yard of medium blue print for binding

3½ yards of fabric for backing

55" x 55" piece of cotton batting

CUTTING

From the assorted light or shirting prints, cut:
- 16 sets of 2 matching squares, 2⅞" x 2⅞" (32 total)
- 16 sets of 5 matching squares, 2½" x 2½" (80 total)

From *each* of the 16 assorted medium or dark print scraps, cut:
- 2 squares, 2⅞" x 2⅞" (32 total)

From the light green print, cut:
- 3 squares, 9¾" x 9¾"; cut each square into quarters diagonally to make 12 setting triangles
- 9 squares, 6½" x 6½"
- 2 squares, 5⅛" x 5⅛"; cut each square in half diagonally to make 4 corner triangles

From the green print, cut on the *lengthwise grain:*
- 2 strips, 3½" x 34½"
- 2 strips, 3½" x 40½"
- 2 strips, 3½" x 43"
- 2 strips, 3½" x 49"

From the medium blue print for middle border, cut:
- 5 strips, 1¾" x 42"

From the medium blue print for binding, cut:
- 6 strips, 2½" x 42"

MAKING THE BLOCKS

For each Double Hourglass block, choose one medium print and one light background print. Some of the light prints may be used more than once. The directions are written for making one block at a time.

1. Draw a diagonal line from corner to corner on the wrong side of two matching light print 2⅞" squares. Layer the marked squares on top of two matching medium or dark print scrap 2⅞" squares, right sides together. Sew ¼" away from the line on both sides. Cut on the drawn line and press the seam allowances toward the darker print. Make four half-square-triangle units.

Make 4.

2. Arrange the four half-square-triangle units together with five matching light print 2½" squares in rows as shown. Sew the rows together to make the Double Hourglass block. Press. Make 16 blocks.

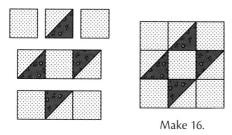

Make 16.

ASSEMBLING THE QUILT TOP

1. Referring to the quilt diagram, lay out the blocks, the light green 6½" squares, and the light green 9¾" side setting triangles together into diagonal rows. Sew the blocks together and press the seam allowances toward the setting pieces. Sew the rows together as shown, pressing the seam allowances in one direction. Add the light green 5⅛" corner triangles and press the seam allowances toward the triangles.

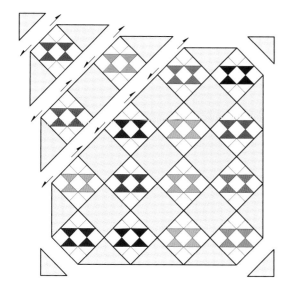

2. Sew the green print 3½" x 34½" strips to the sides of the quilt top. Press the seam allowances toward the border. Sew the green print 3½" x 40½" strips to the top and bottom of the quilt. Press.

3. Sew the five medium blue 1¾" x 42" strips together into one long length. Cut into two strips, 40½" long, and two strips, 43" long. Sew the 1¾" x 40½" strips to the sides of the quilt top. Press the seam allowances toward the blue border.

Sew the 1¾" x 43" strips to the top and bottom of the quilt. Press toward the blue border.

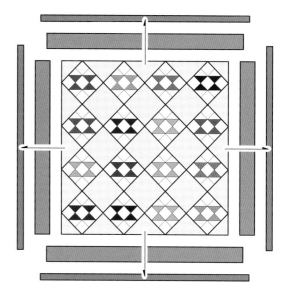

4. Sew the green print 3½" x 43" strips to the sides of the quilt top. Press the seam allowances toward the border. Sew the green print 3½" x 49" strips to the top and bottom of the quilt. Press toward the border.

FINISHING THE QUILT

1. Layer the quilt top, batting, and backing; baste the layers together as shown in "Putting the Quilt Together" (page 75).

2. This quilt was machine quilted with a feathered-wreath design in the setting blocks, quilted in the ditch along the Double Hourglass blocks, and quilted with a feather motif in the borders.

3. Attach the binding to the quilt, referring to "Binding" (page 76).

Shoo-Fly Doll Quilt

Finished quilt: 22" x 27½"
Finished block: 4½" x 4½"

A shoofly was a child's rocker first made in the 1860s. It had a seat built between supports that typically represented an animal figure. This little quilted treasure was inspired by imagining how many women found comfort in watching children in their daily play, while they quilted or rocked in their own chairs, waiting endlessly for the war to be over.

MATERIALS

Yardage is based on 42"-wide, 100% cotton fabric.

⅜ yard *total* of 6 assorted light and shirting prints for blocks

⅓ yard of brown print for border

¼ yard of pink print for sashing

¼ yard *total* of 6 assorted pink prints for blocks and border corner squares

¼ yard *total* of 6 assorted brown prints for blocks and sashing squares

¼ yard of pink print for binding

¾ yard of fabric for backing

26" x 32" piece of thin cotton batting

CUTTING

From *each* of the 6 assorted light prints, cut:
- 4 squares, 2⅜" x 2⅜" (24 total)
- 8 squares, 2" x 2" (48 total)

From *each* of the 6 assorted brown prints for blocks and sashing squares, cut:
- 2 squares, 2⅜" x 2⅜" (12 total)
- 1 square, 2" x 2" (6 total)

From *each* of the 6 assorted pink prints for blocks and border corner squares, cut:
- 2 squares, 2⅜" x 2⅜" (12 total)
- 1 square, 2" x 2" (6 total)

From the pink print for sashing, cut:
- 3 strips, 1½" x 42"; cut into 17 rectangles, 1½" x 5"

From *1* of the assorted brown prints, cut:
- 6 squares, 1½" x 1½"

From the brown print for border, cut:
- 2 strips, 3½" x 42"; cut each strip into 1 strip, 3½" x 16", and 1 strip, 3½" x 21½"

From *1* of the assorted pink prints, cut:
- 4 squares, 3½" x 3½"

From the pink print for binding, cut:
- 3 strips, 1¼" x 42"

MAKING THE BLOCKS

The instructions are written for making one Shoo-Fly block at a time.

1. Layer two matching light print 2⅜" squares on top of two matching pink print 2⅜" squares, right sides together. Draw a diagonal line from corner to corner on the wrong side of each light square. Stitch ¼" from the line on both sides and cut on the drawn line. Press the seam allowances toward the pink fabric. Make four half-square-triangle units.

Make 4.

2. Arrange the four units from step 1, a matching pink 2" square, and four matching light 2" squares together in rows as shown. Sew the rows together to make the block. Press the seam allowances as shown. Make a total of six pink blocks and six brown blocks.

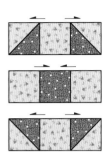

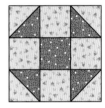

Make 6 pink blocks
and 6 brown blocks.

ASSEMBLING THE QUILT TOP

1. Sew three blocks together with two pink print 1½" x 5" sashing rectangles to make a row, alternating pink and brown blocks. Press toward the sashing. Make four rows.

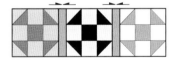

Make 4.

2. Sew three pink print 1½" x 5" sashing rectangles together with two brown print 1½" sashing squares to make a sashing row. Press toward the sashing. Make three.

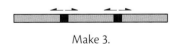

Make 3.

3. Sew the block rows and sashing rows together as shown, pressing the seam allowances toward the sashing rows.

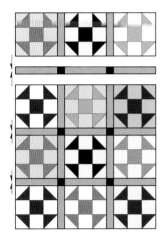

4. Sew the brown print 3½" x 21½" strips to the sides of the quilt and press the seam allowances toward the borders. Sew a pink print 3½" square to each end of both brown print 3½" x 16" border strips and press the seam allowances toward the border strip. Sew these to the top and bottom of the quilt and press.

FINISHING THE QUILT

1. Layer the quilt top, batting, and backing; baste the layers together as shown in "Putting the Quilt Together" (page 75).
2. I quilted diagonal lines across the blocks and diagonal lines in the opposite direction in the borders.
3. Attach the binding to the quilt, referring to "Single-Fold Binding" (page 77).

SEWING FOR THE CAUSE

April 1862

Sewing societies were organized long ago and every neighborhood has
one. Ours meets first at one house and then at another, and all of us sew
steadily all day long. Mother cuts many of the garments and Mrs. Manning
helps her, that is, when they meet with us.

~Diary of Susan Bradford Eppes

May 1861

Many of the young men are going from Canandaigua and all the neighboring towns. It seems very patriotic and grand when they are singing, "It is sweet, Oh, 'tis sweet, for one's country to die," and we hear the martial music and see the flags flying and see the recruiting tents on the square and meet men in uniform at every turn and see train loads of the boys in blue going to the front, but it will not seem so grand if we hear they are dead on the battlefield, far from home. A lot of us girls went down to the train and took flowers to the soldiers as they were passing through and they cut buttons from their coats and gave to us as souvenirs. We have flags on our paper and envelopes, and have all our stationery bordered with red, white and blue. We wear little flag pins for badges and tie our hair with red, white and blue ribbon and have pins and earrings made of the buttons the soldiers gave us. We are going to sew for them in our society and get the garments all cut from the older ladies' society. They work every day in one of the rooms of the courthouse and cut out garments and make them and scrape lint and roll up bandages. They say they will provide us with all the garments we will make. We are going to write notes and enclose them in the garments to cheer up the soldier boys.

    It does not seem now as though I could give up anyone who belonged to me. The girls in our society say that if any of the members do send a soldier to the war they shall have a flag bed quilt, made by the society, and have the girls' names on the stars.

~Diary of Caroline Cowles Clarke

There was a strong connection between women's sewing and the reform work they carried out during the war and even before the war began. In 1861, when war broke out, great numbers of women went to work to organize their church groups and sewing circles into supporting the war effort. In response to Lincoln's call for volunteers, ladies aid societies sprang up across the country, collecting food and supplies for soldiers and making clothes, quilts, blankets, and "comfortables" as well as knitted items for those who enlisted.

The United States Sanitary Commission was founded in 1861 at the beginning of the war. Its purpose was to promote clean and healthy conditions in the Union Army camps. The Commission, aided by thousands of women, staffed field hospitals, raised money, provided supplies, and worked to educate the military and government on matters of health and sanitation. It is believed that the organization cut the disease rate of the Union Army by half and raised about $25 million in support of the Northern war effort. According to Pat Ferrero in *Hearts and Hands,* it is estimated that women supplied the Commission with as many as 250,000 quilts and comforts (a tied quilt with heavy batting), distributed to soldiers in camps or hospitals. Sanitary Fairs were created to raise money to purchase medical supplies and to help ease the suffering of Union soldiers. The fairs, organized by thousands of women volunteers, were extremely popular and often raised more funds than expected—in some cases the equivalent of $4 million today.

July 1862

Three days of each week are devoted to sewing for the soldiers. Often we sew steadily for days at a time, that is when we are getting up a special box to be sent by some soldier, who has been on a visit home and is returning to camp. Cousin Henry Bradford will take the box we are making ready now, he is a Major and certainly looks handsome in his beautiful uniform, just a single star on his collar and chevrons on his sleeves.

~*Diary of Susan Bradford Eppes*

Scrap Squares Doll Quilt

Finished quilt: 17½" x 22¾"
Finished block: 4" x 4"

Seeing scraps of fabric piled in a basket makes my creative spirit soar and I am often pulled to make something, anything, from these scrap pieces. I'd like to believe that women of the past were inspired to make quilts in this way too. This little doll quilt is a perfect example of an easy way to use up some of your scraps or charm packs. It's so quick—make one for yourself and one for a friend!

MATERIALS

Yardage is based on 42"-wide, 100% cotton fabric.

¼ yard of light shirting print for sashing

12 different charm squares* or scraps, at least 4½" x 4½", for blocks

⅛ yard *total* of assorted medium or dark print scraps, at least 1¾" x 1¾" for sashing squares

¼ yard of red print for binding

¾ yard of fabric for backing

22" x 27" piece of thin cotton batting

Charm squares are precut squares measuring 5" x 5".

CUTTING

From *each* assorted charm square or scrap, cut:

- 1 square, 4½" x 4½" (12 total)

From the light shirting print, cut:

- 4 strips, 1¾" x 42"; cut into 31 rectangles, 1¾" x 4½"

From the assorted medium or dark scrap prints, cut:

- 20 squares, 1¾" x 1¾"

From the red print, cut:

- 3 strips, 1¼" x 42"

ASSEMBLING THE QUILT TOP

1. Sew three 4½" squares together with four light 1¾" x 4½" sashing rectangles to make a row. Press seam allowances toward the squares. Make four rows.

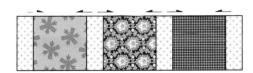

Make 4.

2. Sew three light sashing rectangles together with four medium or dark 1¾" squares to make a sashing row. Press the seam allowances toward the squares. Make five rows.

Make 5.

3. Sew the quilt together as shown.

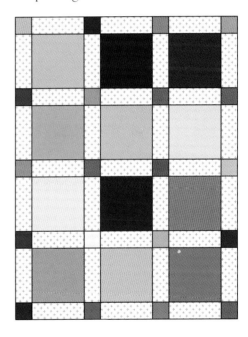

FINISHING THE QUILT

1. Layer the quilt top, batting, and backing, and pin or baste the layers together as shown in "Putting the Quilt Together" (page 75).

2. This quilt was machine quilted with a simple diagonal crosshatch pattern using brown thread.

3. Attach the binding to the quilt, referring to "Single-Fold Binding" (page 77).

Civil War Stars Doll Quilt

Finished quilt: 19½" x 19½"
Finished block: 4" x 4"

According to the January 26, 1861, edition of Harper's Weekly, *the first shots of the Civil War were actually fired by South Carolina on January 10, 1861, at the Union ship, Star of the West, as it was on its way with men and supplies to reinforce Fort Sumter. The war that ensued in the next few months revived a spirit of patriotism in the nation as well as a devotion to the flag and its symbols.*

MATERIALS

Yardage is based on 42"-wide, 100% cotton fabric.

⅛ yard *total* of assorted red, blue, gold and shirting prints for star blocks

¼ yard of medium blue print for outer border

⅛ yard of dark blue print for inner border

1 piece, 5" x 5", *each of 4 red prints for star points**

1 piece, 5" x 5", *each of 4 blue prints for star points**

1 piece, 5" x 5", *of gold print for star points**

¼ yard of red print for binding

¾ yard of fabric for backing

24" x 24" piece of thin cotton batting

*Precut 5" x 5" pieces are known as charm squares.

CUTTING

From *each* of the 4 assorted red prints for star points, cut:

- 8 squares, 1½" x 1½" (32 total)

From *each* of the 4 assorted blue prints for star points, cut:

- 8 squares, 1½" x 1½" (32 total)

From the gold print for star points, cut:

- 8 squares, 1½" x 1½"

From the assorted red, blue, gold, and shirting prints, cut:

- 9 sets of 4 matching rectangles, 1½" x 2½"
- 9 sets of 4 matching squares, 1½" x 1½"
- 36 squares, 1½" x 1½"

From the dark blue print for inner border, cut:

- 2 strips, 1¼" x 42"; cut into 2 strips, 1¼" x 12½", and 2 strips, 1¼" x 14"

From the medium blue print for outer border, cut:

- 2 strips, 3 " x 42"; cut into 2 strips, 3" x 14", and 2 strips, 3" x 19"

From the red print for binding, cut:

- 3 strips, 1¼" x 42"

MAKING THE BLOCKS

The best way to put this scrappy little quilt together is to make one block at a time using a variety of red, blue, gold, and light shirting print scraps. Some prints may be used more than once. There are four stars with red points, four stars with blue points, and one star with gold points placed in the center of the quilt.

1. Sew four assorted print or shirting 1½" squares together as shown to make two units. Press, and then sew the two units together to make a four-patch unit for the center of the block.

2. Choose eight matching 1½" squares for the star points. Draw a diagonal line on the wrong side of each square. Layer a marked square on one end of an assorted print or shirting 1½" x 2½" rectangle. Stitch on the diagonal line as shown. Trim to a ¼" seam allowance. Flip and press the seam allowance toward the corner. Place another marked square on the other end of the rectangle and repeat. Make four flying-geese units. Press.

Make 4.

3. Sew a matching 1½" square to each end of two of the flying-geese units. Press. Sew the remaining two flying-geese units to the sides of the four-patch unit from step 1 as shown. Sew the rows together to make the block. Make nine blocks: four with red star points, four with blue star points, and one with gold star points.

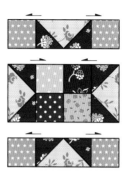 

Make 9.

ASSEMBLING THE QUILT TOP

1. Sew the blocks together into three rows of three blocks each, as shown, alternating stars with red points and blue points and placing the star with gold points in the center. Press the seam allowances in the opposite direction from row to row. Sew the rows together and press the seam allowances in one direction.

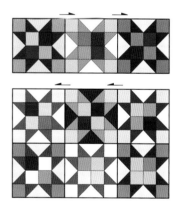

2. Sew the dark blue 1¼" x 12½" strips to the sides of the quilt top, pressing the seam allowances

toward the border. Sew the dark blue 1¼" x 14" strips to the top and bottom of the quilt and press.

3. Sew the medium blue 3" x 14" strips to the sides of the quilt top, pressing the seam allowances toward the outer border. Sew the medium blue 3" x 19" strips to the top and bottom of the quilt top and press.

FINISHING THE QUILT

1. Layer the quilt top, batting, and backing, and baste the layers together as shown in "Putting the Quilt Together" (page 75).
2. The quilt shown was machine quilted with a simple X in the center of each the stars. It was quilted in the ditch along the inside edge of the inner border and through the middle of the outer border.
3. Attach the binding to the quilt, referring to "Single-Fold Binding" (page 77).

Soldier's Cot Quilt

Machine quilted by Dawn Larsen.

Finished quilt: 54" x 79"

Finished block: 12½" x 12½"

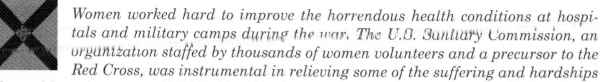

Women worked hard to improve the horrendous health conditions at hospitals and military camps during the war. The U.S. Sanitary Commission, an organization staffed by thousands of women volunteers and a precursor to the Red Cross, was instrumental in relieving some of the suffering and hardships that soldiers faced. Cot-sized quilts were particularly in demand to combat the shortage of suitable bedding and the quicker they could be made the better. Of more than 250,000 quilts that were made for and distributed to Union soldiers, only a few exist today. This easy-to-piece quilt was inspired by one that's displayed at the Lincoln Memorial Shrine in Redlands, California, and is also similar to one used by the Home of the Brave Quilt Project in their efforts to distribute Civil War reproduction quilts to honor present-day soldiers and their families.

MATERIALS

Yardage is based on 42"-wide, 100% cotton fabric.

2 yards of a brown print for outer border

⅛ yard *each* of 15 assorted Civil War reproduction prints for block Xs

15 pieces, 12" x 12" of assorted Civil War reproduction prints for block backgrounds

15 pieces, 3" x 3" of assorted Civil War reproduction prints for block centers

½ yard of teal print for inner border

⅝ yard of dark blue print for binding

4⅞ yards of fabric for backing

60" x 85" piece of cotton batting

15" square ruler

CUTTING

From *each* of the 15 assorted reproduction prints for block backgrounds, cut:

- 1 square, 11" x 11"; cut into quarters diagonally to make 4 triangles (60 total)

From *each* of the 15 assorted reproduction prints for block Xs, cut:

- 1 strip, 2⅝" x 42"; cut into 4 rectangles, 2⅝" x 9" (60 total)

From *each* of the 15 assorted reproduction prints for block centers, cut:

- 1 square, 2⅝" x 2⅝" (15 total)

From the teal print, cut:

- 6 strips, 2½" x 42"

From the brown print, cut on the *lengthwise grain*:

- 2 strips, 6½" x 54"
- 2 strips, 6½" x 67"

From the dark blue binding print, cut:

- 7 strips, 2½" x 42"

MAKING THE BLOCKS

For each X block, choose four matching 2⅝" x 9" rectangles, four matching triangles for the background, and a 2⅝" square for the center.

1. Sew a triangle to each side of two 2⅝" x 9" rectangles. Press. Make two units.

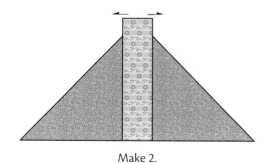

Make 2.

2. Sew the remaining two 2⅝" x 9" rectangles to each side of a 2⅝" square. Press.

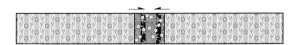

3. Sew the two units from step 1 together with the unit from step 2 as shown. Referring to "Pressing Pointers" at right, press the seam allowances as desired.

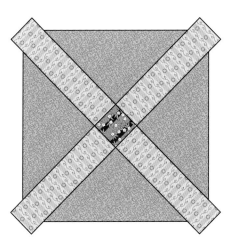

4. Place the 6½" point of a square rule in the center of the block. Trim the sides of the block. Rotate the block 180° and trim to 13" square. Make a total of 15 blocks.

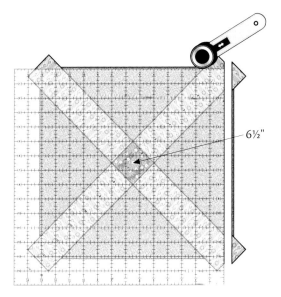

6½"

Pressing Pointers

You may want to press the seam allowances open for these blocks to make quilt-top assembly easier. Sew with a shorter stitch length if you choose this option. You can also press the seam allowances of seven of the blocks in the opposite direction so that the seams will butt together. This will limit your ability to juggle blocks around in the final arrangement, but the seams will be easy to match.

ASSEMBLING THE QUILT TOP

1. Sew three of the blocks together into a row. Make five rows. Press the seam allowances in opposite directions from row to row. Sew the rows together and press.

2. Sew the six teal 2½" x 42" strips together to make one long strip. Cut two strips, 2½" x 63", and sew them to the sides of the quilt top. Press the seam allowances toward the border.

3. Cut the remaining teal strip into two strips, 2½" x 42", and sew them to the top and bottom of the quilt. Press toward the border.

4. Sew the two brown 6½" x 67" strips to the sides of the quilt top. Press the seam allowances toward the outer border. Add the brown 6½" x 54" strips to the top and bottom of the quilt. Press toward the outer border.

FINISHING THE QUILT

1. Layer the quilt top, batting, and backing; baste the layers together as shown in "Putting the Quilt Together" (page 75).

2. This quilt was machine quilted with an allover stipple pattern.

3. Attach the binding to the quilt, referring to "Binding" (page 76).

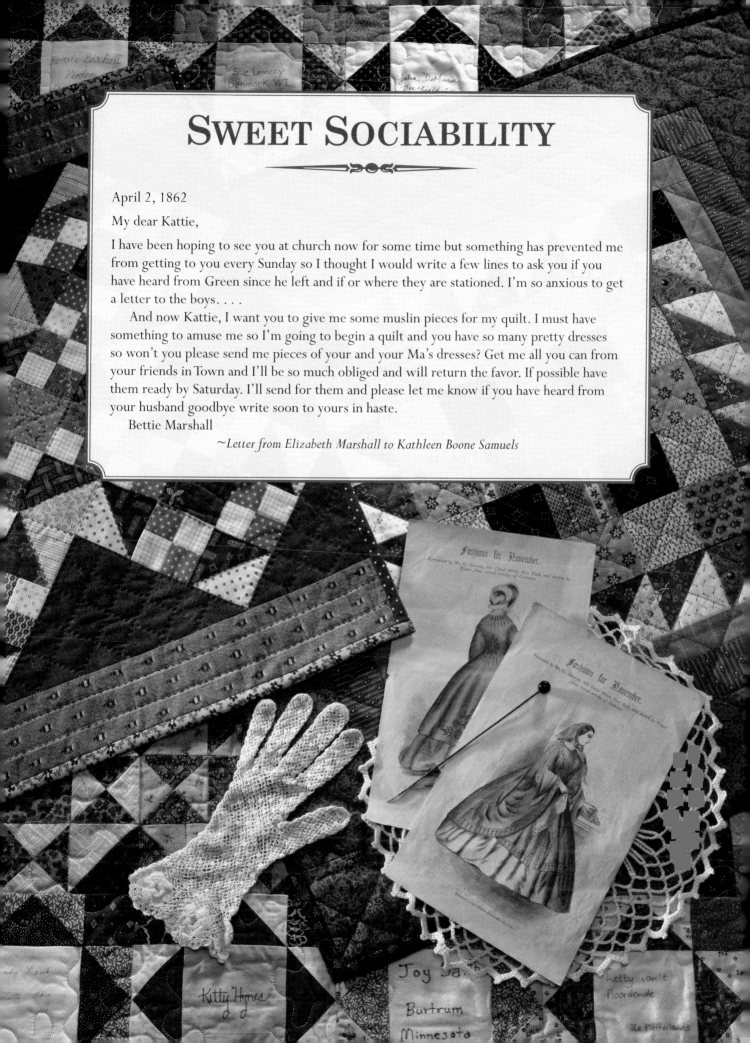

SWEET SOCIABILITY

April 2, 1862

My dear Kattie,

I have been hoping to see you at church now for some time but something has prevented me from getting to you every Sunday so I thought I would write a few lines to ask you if you have heard from Green since he left and if or where they are stationed. I'm so anxious to get a letter to the boys. . . .

And now Kattie, I want you to give me some muslin pieces for my quilt. I must have something to amuse me so I'm going to begin a quilt and you have so many pretty dresses so won't you please send me pieces of your and your Ma's dresses? Get me all you can from your friends in Town and I'll be so much obliged and will return the favor. If possible have them ready by Saturday. I'll send for them and please let me know if you have heard from your husband goodbye write soon to yours in haste.

Bettie Marshall

~Letter from Elizabeth Marshall to Kathleen Boone Samuels

August 24, 1861

I should have been cheerful in my solitude, had it not been for my irrepressible anxiety about public affairs.

   I made, and quilted on my lap, the prettiest little crib-quilt you ever saw. The outside had ninety-nine little pink stars of French calico, on a white ground, with a rose-wreath trimming all round for a border; and the lining was a very delicate rose-colored French brilliant. It took one month of industrious sewing to complete it. I sent it to my dear friend, Mrs. S., in honor of her first granddaughter. It was really a relief to my mind to be doing something for an innocent little baby in these dreadful times.

~*Letter from Lydia Maria Child to Henrietta Sargent*

One of the most difficult aspects of the war for women may have been the waiting and worrying, learning news of the dead or wounded loved ones from newspapers or letters. It was likely that women used their social networks as a means to survive the stress and strain of the war. Many women also may have taken to their needles as a way to sustain themselves through their anguish and grief. Since sewing was often at the center of much of women's community involvement during the nineteenth century, engaging in charitable activities through these circles or "quiltings," as they were sometimes called, may very well have helped ease some of the anxiety many women faced as their husbands, sons, fathers, brothers, and loved ones went to war.

   In order to bear the burden of being left on the home front and to withstand living in the midst of such turmoil, women had to find ways to pass the

time. We need only look at quilts like the one made by Jane A. Stickle, the famous "Dear Jane" quilt, containing 225 blocks and 5,602 pieces, to see examples of how women kept their worries at bay by keeping their hands and minds busy. The craving for companionship many of these women may have felt as their world was turned upside down becomes evident. Trading news and stories in a community with others in the same situations, women formed and strengthened bonds to get them through the difficult times.

Women organized themselves into groups to contribute sewn items for the war. In addition to sewing quilts, some groups focused on contributing a specific item needed by the troops. So there were not only sock and slipper circles, but knitting and handkerchief circles as well. The reciprocal love and support women received from friends and family members may have played a crucial part in their well being during this critical time. Much of the same reciprocal love and support fuels quilting guilds today and, just as they did during the Civil War, women find not only companionship, but also a certain solace that these groups provide members.

Packages that were sent to soldiers through ladies aid societies sometimes arrived with notes:

"My dear friend, You are not my husband or son, but you are the husband or son of some woman who undoubtedly loves you as I love mine. I have made these garments for you with a heart that sews for your sufferings."

~From Spicer, History of the Ninth and Tenth Regiments

"My son is in the army. Whoever is made warm with this quilt, which I have worked on for six days and the greater part of six nights, let him remember his own mother's love."

~From Hackett, Christian Memorials of the War

"This blanket was carried by Millie Aldrich, who is ninety-three years old, downhill and uphill, one and a half miles, to be given to some soldier."

~From Hackett, Christian Memorials of the War

Civil War Scraps Doll Quilt

Finished quilt: 17½" x 22"
Finished block: 6" x 6"

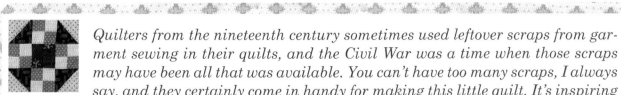

Quilters from the nineteenth century sometimes used leftover scraps from garment sewing in their quilts, and the Civil War was a time when those scraps may have been all that was available. You can't have too many scraps, I always say, and they certainly come in handy for making this little quilt. It's inspiring to play with small pieces of fabric, and sometimes you can come up with a pleasing quilt using a very simple design in no time at all.

MATERIALS

Yardage is based on 42"-wide, 100% cotton fabric.

⅛ yard *total* of 5 assorted medium and dark Civil War reproduction prints for blocks

⅛ yard *total* of 5 assorted light prints for four-patch units

⅛ yard *total* of 5 assorted light prints for block backgrounds

⅛ yard *total* of 5 assorted medium blue prints for four-patch units

⅓ yard or 1 fat quarter of dark blue print for setting triangles

⅛ yard of green print for borders

5 pieces, 3" x 3", of red, blue, or green Civil War reproduction prints for block centers

⅛ yard of red print for binding

⅛ yard of blue print for binding

⅝ yard of fabric for backing

22" x 26" piece of thin cotton batting

CUTTING

From *each* of the 5 assorted light prints for block backgrounds, cut:

- 2 squares, 2⅞" x 2⅞" (10 total)

From *each* of the 5 assorted medium and dark reproduction prints, cut:

- 2 squares, 2⅞" x 2⅞" (10 total)

From *each* of the 5 red, blue, or green reproduction prints, cut:

- 1 square, 2½" x 2½" (5 total)

From *each* of the 5 assorted light prints for four-patch units, cut:

- 8 squares, 1½" x 1½" (40 total)

From *each* of the 5 assorted medium blue prints, cut:

- 8 squares, 1½" x 1½" (40 total)

From the dark blue print, cut:

- 1 square, 9¾" x 9¾"; cut into quarters diagonally to make 4 triangles
- 2 squares, 5⅛" x 5⅛"; cut in half diagonally to make 4 triangles

From the green print, cut:

- 2 strips, 2¾" x 17½"

From the red print for binding, cut:

- 2 strips, 1¼" x 23"

From the blue print for binding, cut:

- 2 strips, 1¼" x 19"

MAKING THE BLOCKS

1. Select two matching light print 2⅞" squares and two matching medium or dark print 2⅞" squares. Layer the light and dark squares right sides together. Draw a diagonal line from corner to corner on the wrong side of each light square. Stitch ¼" from the line on both sides and cut on the drawn line. Press the seam allowances toward the darker fabric. Make four half-square-triangle units.

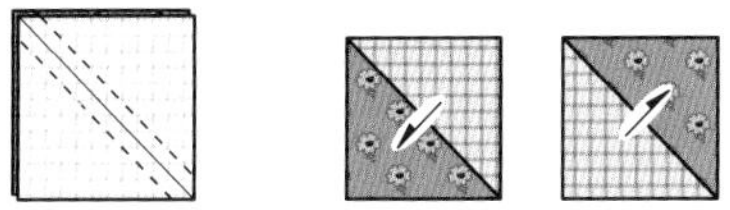

Make 4.

2. Sew two matching light print 1½" squares and two matching medium blue print 1½" squares together as shown. Make four matching four-patch units.

Make 4.

3. Assemble the block by sewing the half-square-triangle units, the four-patch units, and a reproduction 2½" square into rows as shown. Press. Sew the rows together. Make a total of five blocks.

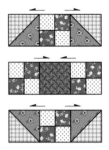
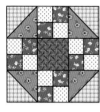

Make 5.

ASSEMBLING THE QUILT TOP

1. Referring to the quilt diagram, lay out the finished blocks and the side setting triangles in diagonal rows. Sew the blocks into rows and press the seam allowances toward the setting pieces. Sew the rows together as shown, pressing the seam allowances in opposite directions. Add the blue print corner triangles and press the seam allowances toward the triangles.

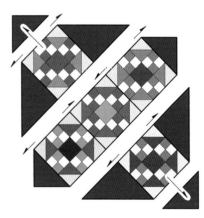

2. Add the medium green strips to the top and bottom of the quilt top. Press the seam allowances toward the border.

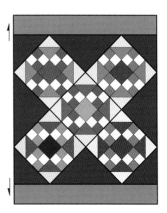

FINISHING THE QUILT

1. Layer the quilt top, batting, and backing; baste the layers together as shown in "Putting the Quilt Together" (page 75).

2. I hand quilted this quilt with a simple design in the center square of the center block and in the ditch along the other blocks. I quilted a crosshatch design in the blue triangles and horizontal lines along the borders.

3. See the box below for instructions on making an overlapped binding with contrasting fabrics.

Making an Overlapped Binding

I used two different fabrics to make the binding on this little quilt. Here's how to do it.

1. Measure the length and width of your quilt, adding 2" to each. Cut two matching binding strips, 1¼"-wide, for the top and bottom and two strips in a contrasting color for the sides of the quilt.

2. Sew the binding to the sides of the quilt using a ¼" seam allowance. Trim the excess length even with the quilt. Hand stitch the binding to the back.

3. Sew the binding to the top and bottom of the quilt, leaving the extra 1" of binding at each end. Trim the ends of the binding to ½" and fold the edges over so that they're even with the bound edge. Pin in place and stitch the binding to the quilt back, securing the corners with extra stitches.

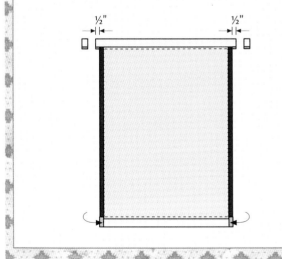

Friendship Album Quilt

Machine quilted by Bonnie Stapleton.
Finished quilt: 48½" x 48½"
Finished block: 6" x 6"

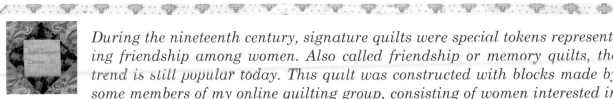

During the nineteenth century, signature quilts were special tokens representing friendship among women. Also called friendship or memory quilts, the trend is still popular today. This quilt was constructed with blocks made by some members of my online quilting group, consisting of women interested in making small quilts and sharing their experiences, ideas, tips, and photos with others. I thought it would be a great idea to have the quilters piece signed Album blocks so that I could make them into a quilt. Many also made Ohio Star blocks, which I incorporated into the design in a medallion style. I've included the pattern here since it fits in nicely with the topic. This is a wonderful quilt to make as a guild project to give to a member or as a special memory quilt for a wedding or anniversary.

MATERIALS

Yardage is based on 42"-wide, 100% cotton fabric.

2½ yards *total* of assorted medium and dark prints for blocks

1⅝ yards *total* of assorted light prints for blocks

½ yard *total* of assorted light prints or muslin for Album block centers

½ yard of red-and-black print for binding

3¼ yards of fabric for backing

53" x 53" piece of cotton batting

Freezer paper

Permanent fine-point fabric pen

CUTTING

For 1 Album Block (Cut 44 total.)

From an assorted medium or dark print for blocks, cut:

- 4 rectangles, 2" x 3½"

From an assorted light print for blocks, cut:

- 8 squares, 2" x 2"

From a *different* assorted medium or dark print for blocks, cut:

- 4 squares, 2" x 2"

From the muslin or light print for Album block centers, cut:

- 1 square, 3½" x 3½"

Cutting for 1 Ohio Star Block (Cut 20 total.)

From an assorted medium or dark print for blocks, cut:

- 2 squares, 2⅞" x 2⅞"; cut in half diagonally to make 4 half-square triangles

From an assorted light print for blocks, cut:

- 2 squares, 2⅞" x 2⅞"; cut in half diagonally to make 4 half-square triangles
- 2 squares, 3¼" x 3¼"; cut into quarters diagonally to make 8 quarter-square triangles

From a *different* assorted medium or dark print for blocks, cut:

- 2 squares, 3¼" x 3¼"; cut into quarters diagonally to make 8 quarter-square triangles
- 1 square, 2½" x 2½"

Cutting for Binding

From the red-and-black print, cut:

- 5 strips, 2½" x 42"

PIECING THE ALBUM BLOCKS

Choose a variety of light, medium, and dark prints to give the quilt a nice contrast after the blocks are pieced together. For each block you will need eight matching light print 2" squares for the flying-geese units, four matching medium or dark print 2" x 3½" rectangles for the flying-geese units, four matching medium or dark print 2" squares for the block corners, and one 3½" light or muslin square for the center.

1. Draw a diagonal line on the wrong side of eight matching light print 2" squares. Layer a marked square on one end of a 2" x 3½" rectangle. Stitch on the diagonal line; trim the corner, leaving a ¼" seam allowance. Flip and press the seam allowance toward the corner. Place a second marked square on the other end of the rectangle, stitch, trim, and press. Make four flying-geese units.

Make 4.

2. Sew a 2" medium or dark print square to both ends of two of the flying-geese units. Sew the other two flying-geese units to the sides of the muslin or light print 3½" square as shown. Sew the rows together to make the block.

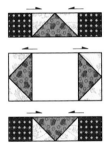

3. Iron a 3" x 3" piece of freezer paper to the back of the muslin or light print square to stabilize it before signing. Use a fine-point, permanent ink pen to sign your name and write any other information you'd like to share. I like to use a Sakura Micron Pigma pen, found at quilt shops or art-supply stores. If you've never used one of these pens before, practice on a piece of scrap fabric first so that you can get a feel for writing on cloth. After signing, remove the freezer paper and press with a warm iron to set the ink.

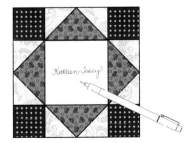

4. Repeat steps 1–3 to make 44 Album blocks.

PIECING THE OHIO STAR BLOCKS

For each Ohio Star block you will need three fabrics: one light and two different mediums or darks.

1. Sew a light print half-square triangle to a medium or dark print half-square triangle. Press the seam allowances toward the darker fabric. Make four half-square-triangle units.

Make 4.

2. Sew a medium or dark quarter-square triangle to a light quarter-square triangle. Press the seam allowances toward the darker fabric. Make eight. Sew the units together in pairs to make four quarter-square-triangle units.

Make 8.   Make 4.

3. Sew the 2½" center square and the units from steps 1 and 2 into rows as shown, pressing the seam allowances in opposite directions from row to row. Sew the rows together and press.

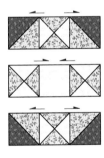

4. Repeat to make a total of 20 blocks.

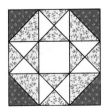

Make 20.

ASSEMBLING THE QUILT TOP

When you are assembling the quilt top, make sure that you place the blocks so that the signatures are all oriented the same

1. Arrange 16 of the Ohio Star blocks into four rows of four blocks each. Sew the blocks together into rows, pressing the seam allowances in opposite directions from row to row. Sew the rows together and press.

2. Arrange eight of the Album blocks into four rows of two blocks as shown. Make two of these units and sew them to the sides of the Ohio Star unit.

3. Sew eight Album blocks together into a row and press. Make two rows. Sew one row to the top of the quilt and one row to the bottom of the quilt and press.

4. Make a row of six Album blocks. Sew an Ohio Star block to each end of the row. Press. Make two rows. Sew one row to the top of the quilt and one row to the bottom of the quilt. Press.

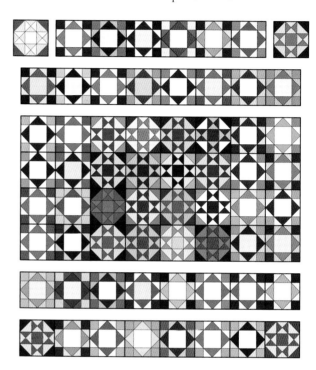

FINISHING THE QUILT

1. Layer the quilt top, batting, and backing; baste the layers together as shown in "Putting the Quilt Together" (page 75).
2. The quilt shown was machine quilted with an all-over stipple design.
3. Attach the binding to the quilt, referring to "Binding" (page 76).

One-Patch Doll Quilt

Finished quilt: 25½" x 25½"
Finished block: 2" x 2"

Centuries ago, young girls learned to sew by practicing their stitches and making small quilts for their dolls. This quilt was inspired by an antique doll quilt I saw that used a variety of scraps cut into simple squares bordered by triangles. It would be perfect for teaching a beginner or child some simple piecing techniques.

MATERIALS

Yardage is based on 42"-wide, 100% cotton fabric.

⅜ yard of dark Civil War reproduction print for outer border

¼ yard of purple print for middle border

⅛ yard of gold print for inner border

⅛ yard *total* of assorted shirting prints for quilt center

⅛ yard *total* of assorted indigo prints for quilt center

6" x 12" scrap *each* of black print and light tan print for quilt center

3" x 6" scrap *each* of blue print, blue striped print, and pink print for quilt center

3" x 3" scrap of gold print for quilt center

¼ yard of black print for binding

⅞ yard of fabric for backing

30" x 30" piece of thin cotton batting

CUTTING

From the black print for quilt center, cut:
- 8 squares, 2½" x 2½"

From the light tan print, cut:
- 8 squares, 2½" x 2½"

From the blue print, cut:
- 4 squares, 2½" x 2½"

From the blue striped print, cut:
- 4 squares, 2½" x 2½"

From the pink print, cut:
- 4 squares, 2½" x 2½"

From the gold print for quilt center, cut:
- 1 square, 2½" x 2½"

From the assorted shirting prints, cut:
- 10 squares, 2⅞" x 2⅞"

From the assorted indigo prints, cut:
- 10 squares, 2⅞" x 2⅞"

From the gold print for inner border, cut:
- 2 strips, 1½" x 14½"
- 2 strips, 1½" x 16½"

From the purple print, cut:
- 2 strips, 2" x 16½"
- 2 strips, 2" x 19½"

From the dark reproduction print, cut:
- 2 strips, 3½" x 19½"
- 2 strips, 3½" x 25½"

From the black print, cut:
- 3 strips, 1¼" x 42"

ASSEMBLING THE QUILT CENTER

1. Using two light tan print 2½" squares, one black print 2½" square, and a blue print 2½" square, make a four-patch unit as shown. Press the seam allowances toward the darker squares. Make four.

Make 4.

2. Sew a pink print 2½" square and a blue striped 2½" square together and press. Make four.

Make 4.

3. Sew two units from step 2 together with the gold print 2½" square as shown. Press.

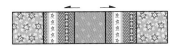

Make 1.

4. Arrange the four-patch units, the units from step 2, and the unit from step 3 as shown. Sew into rows. Press. Join the rows to make the center of the quilt top.

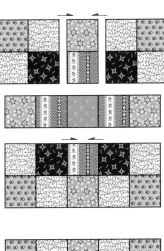

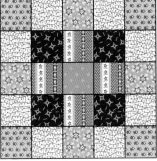

5. Draw a diagonal line from corner to corner on the wrong side of each shirting 2⅞" square. Layer a marked square on top of an indigo 2⅞" square, right sides together. Stitch ¼" from the line on both sides and cut on the drawn line. Press the seam allowances toward the darker fabric. Make 20 half-square-triangle units.

Make 20.

6. Sew five half-square-triangle units together into a strip. Press. Make four strips.

Make 4.

7. Sew two of the strips from step 5 to the sides of the quilt top, arranging them as shown. Press. Sew a black print 2½" square to each end of the remaining two half-square-triangle strips and press. Sew these to the top and bottom of the quilt top and press.

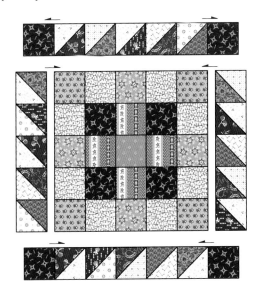

ASSEMBLING THE QUILT TOP

1. Sew the gold print 1½" x 14½" strips to the sides of the quilt top and press the seam allowances toward the border. Add the two gold print 1½" x 16½" strips to the top and bottom of the quilt top. Press.

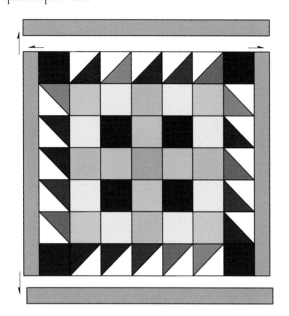

2. Sew the purple print 2" x 16½" strips to the sides of the quilt top and press the seam allowances toward the border. Add the two purple print 2" x 19½" strips to the top and bottom of the quilt top. Press toward the border.

3. Sew the dark print 3½" x 19½" strips to the sides of the quilt top and press the seam allowances toward the border. Add the two dark print 2" x 25½" strips to the top and bottom of the quilt top. Press toward the border.

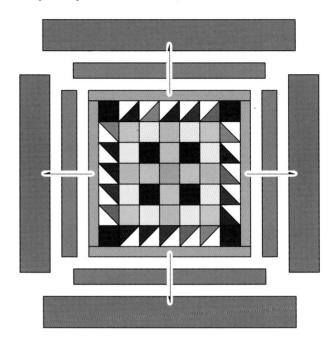

FINISHING THE QUILT

1. Layer the quilt top, batting, and backing; pin or baste the layers together as shown in "Putting the Quilt Together" (page 75).
2. This quilt was machine quilted with a simple cross-hatching design.
3. Attach the binding to the quilt, referring to "Single-Fold Binding" (page 77).

TOKENS OF AFFECTION

Harpers Ferry
June 10th, 1861

My Dear Sister

. . . I received your kind present, the covering for the head; it was the admiration of all the boys who declared the sewing excellent. Many questions were asked me about it and particularly who the seamstress was. Oh Kattie you have no idea how that dear little present touched my heart, it seemed to breathe such a spirit of love for me and consideration for my bodily comfort. . . .

You will also find my sleeve buttons enclosed; they are of no use to me here and will be safer with you. You will please keep both badge and sleeve buttons as your own should I never have use for them again. . . .

Yours Sincerely
G. B. Samuels

~Letter from Green Berry Samuels to Kathleen Boone Samuels

Gettysburg
July 3, 1863

Can my prettice* do patchwork? If she can, she must piece together these penciled scraps of soiled paper and make out of them, not a log-cabin quilt, but a wren's nest, cement it with love and fill it with blue and golden and speckled eggs of faith and hope, to hatch out a greater love yet for us. . . . The suffering and waiting are almost unbearable. . . .

Well, my sweetheart, at one o'clock the awful silence was broken by a cannon-shot and then another, and then more than a hundred guns shook the hills from crest to base, answered by more than another hundred—the whole world a blazing volcano, the whole of heaven a thunderbolt—then darkness and absolute silence—then the grim and gruesome, low-spoken commands—then the forming of the attacking columns. My brave Virginians are to attack in front. Oh, may God in mercy help me as He never helped before. . . .

Now, I go; but remember always that I love you with all my heart and soul, with every fiber of my being; that now and forever I am yours—yours, my beloved. It is almost three o'clock. My soul reaches out to yours—my prayers. . . .

Your Soldier

~General Pickett's letter to his sweetheart, Sallie, right before he led the charge on the last day of the Battle of Gettysburg.

*"Prettice" is a term of affection used throughout his letters.

Manassas Junction
October 11, 1861

Dear Mother:

I would have written as soon as I received your letter if the box had come with it, but as the captain could not bring them with him, he had to get them transported on freight, which did not arrive until yesterday. . . .

    I am thankful for the boots, which are a trifle too large but I reckon by the time that I put on two or three pairs of stockings, they will nearly fit me. We were all very glad to see the captain and we were also pleased to see the things he brought with him, which added so much to our comfort. Times are all very quiet about here. We hear firing on the Potomac nearly every day, though I heard some of the boys say that Mr. Christman was collecting goods to bring to the soldiers. If such be the case I wish you would send me an old quilt or something as somebody has stolen my shawl and I think I shall need one this winter, but you need not send anything unless someone can bring it, for it will cost too much to get anything here. . . .

    I must close now, give my love to all and tell them to write.
    Goodbye.

Your loving son,
George
~Letter from George Lee to his mother

I find it fascinating to see history unfold upon the pages of some of the letters written during the war, something that is often left out of the history books. Love letters were frequently the most sincere token of affection during the nineteenth century. While they often contain accounts of camp life, battles that were endured, and other struggles the men faced, many are also laced with affection and steadfast devotion. Along with jewelry, a lock of hair, or photographs, love letters were perhaps the most personal tokens of all and offered the strongest connection to home and loved ones. And if the men who wrote them did not return, the letters still remained, lasting legacies of love.

Pillow Pincushion

Finished pincushion: 3½" x 4½"

Young girls learned to sew and practiced their stitches by making small quilts for their dolls. Wouldn't this cute little doll pillow pincushion make a great accessory to display next to your small quilts? It's also perfect to make for a friendship exchange or as a small gift or token for your sewing friends.

MATERIALS

1 piece, 6" x 9", of striped ticking fabric
1 piece, 5" x 9", of blue print for pillowcase
¼ yard of eyelet or lace trim, 1¼" to 1½" wide
Polyfil or poly beads for stuffing

CUTTING

From the blue print, cut:
- 1 rectangle, 3¾" x 8"

From the piece of eyelet or lace trim, cut:
- 1 strip, 8" long

From the striped ticking fabric, cut:
- 1 rectangle, 5" x 8"

MAKING THE PINCUSHION

1. With right sides together and using a ¼" seam, sew the eyelet or lace trim to the blue print rectangle along the right-hand long side. Press open. Press the seam allowances toward the blue print. Topstitch ⅛" away from the seam.

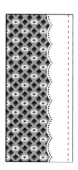

2. Layer the pillowcase unit (right side up) on top of the right side of the striped ticking rectangle as shown. Align the raw edges on the left side; the right side will extend approximately ½" beyond the pillowcase unit. Fold the layered pieces together in half with right sides together.

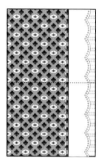

3. Stitch ¼" around the folded piece, leaving a 2" opening for turning on the long side. Trim the seam allowances along the fold and at the corners.

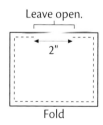

4. Turn the pillow right side out and stuff with either polyfil or poly beads for more weight. Slip-stitch the opening closed.

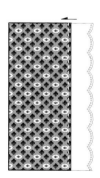
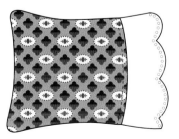

Pink Patches Doll Quilt

Finished quilt: 17½" x 21¾"
Finished block: 3" x 3"

Years ago, children hand pieced squares for doll quilts at an early age, learning valuable sewing skills as they went along. I really love playing with scrap squares and the simple Four Patch blocks in this antique-looking doll quilt, and the wonderful blend of pink and brown prints make it one of my favorites. If you have ever considered hand quilting, this is a great little quilt to practice on.

MATERIALS

Yardage is based on 42"-wide, 100% cotton fabric.

¼ yard of pink print for setting squares

¼ yard of dark brown print for setting triangles

¼ yard *total* of assorted light prints for Four Patch blocks

¼ yard *total* of assorted medium prints for Four Patch blocks

¼ yard of pink print for binding

¾ yard of fabric for backing

22" x 26" piece of cotton batting

CUTTING

From the assorted light prints, cut:

- 40 squares, 2" x 2", in matching sets of two

From the assorted medium prints, cut:

- 40 squares, 2" x 2", in matching sets of two

From the pink print for setting squares, cut:

- 12 squares, 3½" x 3½"

From the dark brown print, cut:

- 4 squares, 5¾" x 5¾"; cut each square into quarters diagonally to make 16 side setting triangles (2 are extra)
- 2 squares, 3¼" x 3¼"; cut each square in half diagonally to make 4 corner triangles

From the pink print for binding, cut:

- 3 strips, 1¼" x 42"

MAKING THE BLOCKS

Choose two matching medium print 2" squares and two matching light print 2" squares. Sew the squares together into rows as shown. Press the seam allowances toward the darker fabric. Sew the rows together to make a Four Patch block. Press. Make 20.

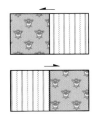

Make 20.

ASSEMBLING THE QUILT TOP

1. Lay out the finished blocks, the pink print 3½" squares, and the dark brown print side setting triangles together into diagonal rows. Sew the blocks, the squares, and the setting triangles into rows, pressing the seam allowances toward the setting squares and triangles. The triangles are cut slightly oversized and will be trimmed later.

2. Sew the rows together, matching the seam intersections. Add the corner triangles and press the seam allowances toward the triangles. Square up the quilt top, making sure to leave ¼" beyond the points of all the blocks for seam allowances.

FINISHING THE QUILT

1. Layer the quilt top, batting, and backing; baste the layers together as shown in "Putting the Quilt Together" (page 75).

2. I hand quilted an orange-peel design in each block.

3. Attach the binding to the quilt, referring to "Single-Fold Binding" (page 77).

Hexagon Flowers Doll Quilt

Finished quilt: 16" x 19½"
Finished block: 3½" x 3½"

This little treasure was inspired by antique hexagon quilts from the nineteenth century. Hexagon quilts, sometimes called Honeycomb or Mosaic quilts, have been around since the early 1800s in America and even earlier than that in England. Many of us today know them as Grandmother's Flower Garden quilts from the thirties. The technique used to prepare and sew the hexagons together is called English paper piecing. The fabric is stitched by hand onto a paper hexagon template. The pieces take a little time to prepare but you'll find they're a perfect take-along project to work on when you have a few minutes here and there. Before you know it, you'll have all the flowers you need to make several little quilts!

MATERIALS

Yardage is based on 42"-wide, 100% cotton fabric.

¼ yard of green print for borders

¼ yard of brown print for block backgrounds

⅛ yard of medium blue print for border corner squares

12 scraps, at least 2" x 12" *each,* of assorted prints for outer hexagons

12 scraps, at least 2" x 2" *each,* of assorted prints for center hexagons

¼ yard of gold print for binding

⅝ yard of fabric for backing

20" x 24" piece of thin cotton batting

Several sheets of cardstock or heavyweight paper for hexagon templates

Single-hole paper punch (optional)

CUTTING

From *each* of the 12 assorted scraps for outer hexagons, cut:
- 6 squares, 2" x 2" (72 total)

From *each* of the 12 assorted scraps for center hexagons, cut:
- 1 square, 2" x 2" (12 total)

From the brown print, cut:
- 12 squares, 4" x 4"

From the green print, cut:
- 2 strips, 3" x 11"
- 2 strips, 3" x 14½"

From the medium blue print, cut:
- 4 squares, 3" x 3"

From the gold print, cut:
- 2 strips, 1¼" x 42"

PREPARING THE HEXAGON TEMPLATES

You will need seven hexagon templates for each flower. I suggest making at least 28 and then using each one three times. To make the hexagon templates, you have several options.

Make your own. Use the pattern (page 58) to make a template. Then trace the template onto cardstock or heavy paper and cut out the hexagons carefully.

Print hexagons from the Internet. I used a website that allows you to print hexagons of any size. Print a grid of hexagons with sides equal to .6"; that's the size I used to create the 3" flowers. Print directly onto cardstock and cut the hexagons apart individually. (The website is http://incompetech.com/graphpaper/hexagonal/.)

Purchase precut paper hexagons. There are several companies that make paper hexagon shapes you can purchase in different sizes to use as templates. You can find them at quilt shops, online, or at quilt shows. Choose hexagon templates that measure ⅝" along the sides, or 1" from flat side to flat side.

After the shapes are cut out, I recommend placing a dot in the center of each paper hexagon and using a single-hole punch to make a hole. The hole makes it easy to pin the templates to the fabric. It also makes it easy to remove the paper templates with the edge of a seam ripper after the pieces have been stitched together.

MAKING THE HEXAGON FLOWER BLOCKS

For each hexagon flower, choose six matching squares for the petals and one contrasting square for the center.

1. Place a paper hexagon in the center on the wrong side of a 2" square. Secure the paper to the fabric by placing a small pin through the hole. Cut around the shape, leaving a generous ¼" all around.

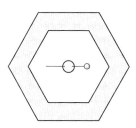

2. Fold one edge over and baste the corner as you fold over the next edge. Go around the hexagon, stitching down all the sides and being careful not to catch the paper. Finish with a knot to secure. Repeat for the six matching hexagons and the contrasting center hexagon. Leave the paper pieces inside.

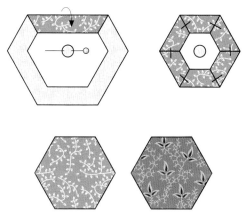

Make 6 matching and 1 contrasting hexagon for each flower.

3. Place the center hexagon right sides together with another hexagon. Whipstitch the sides together, catching just the edges of the fabric.

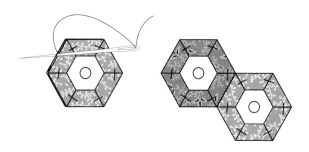

4. Continue adding the remaining hexagons around the edges of the center hexagon in a circular fashion.

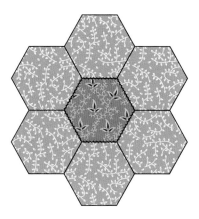

5. Connect the sides of the outer hexagons by placing them right sides together, folding the paper if necessary. When you've finished a flower, remove the paper hexagons and press flat.

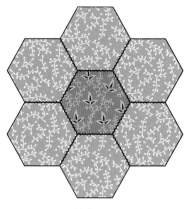

Make 12.

6. Repeat steps 1–5 to make 12 hexagon flowers, reusing the paper templates as desired.

7. Center and appliqué a hexagon flower to each brown print 4" square. Make 12.

Make 12.

ASSEMBLING THE QUILT TOP

1. Sew three blocks together to make a row. Press. Make four rows. Sew the rows together.

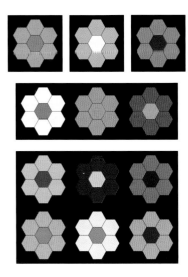

2. Sew the green print 3" x 14½" strips to the sides of the quilt. Press the seam allowances toward the borders. Sew a medium blue 3" square to each end

of both green 3" x 11" strips and press toward the strips. Sew these to the top and bottom of the quilt top and press toward the border.

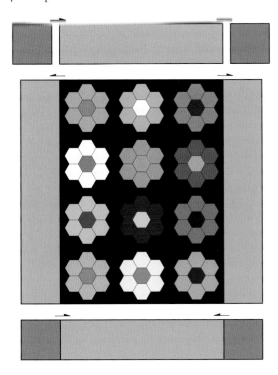

FINISHING THE QUILT

1. Layer the quilt top, batting, and backing; pin or baste the layers together as shown in "Putting the Quilt Together" (page 75).

2. I hand quilted in the ditch around the blocks and quilted straight lines in the border.

3. Attach the binding to the quilt, referring to "Single-Fold Binding" (page 77).

Hexagon

Civil War Letter Pocket and Needle Case

Finished letter pocket: 4½" x 7½"
Finished needle case: 3" x 4½"

We can only imagine how eagerly women awaited letters from their husbands or loved ones who were fighting in the Civil War. I wonder if they kept the letters in a safe place nearby while they were sewing, in their sewing baskets perhaps, taking them out often to read and reread.

Needle cases were appreciated by men as they went off to war since soldiers relied on their contents (needles, thread, and buttons) to prepare for Sunday morning inspections and because they also had to mend their own uniforms in the camps and out on the field. Try making these accessories in muted colors or in a patriotic print to give them a real historical feel and show off your Civil War reproduction fabrics.

MATERIALS

Materials for Letter Pocket

1 fat eighth of Civil War reproduction print for cover
1 fat eighth of Civil War reproduction print for lining
7¾" x 12¾" piece of interfacing
Button and/or snap (optional)

Materials for Needle Case

7" x 10" scrap of Civil War reproduction print for
   cover
7" x 10" scrap of Civil War reproduction print for
   lining
4¾" x 8¼" piece of interfacing
2" x 3" piece of wool felt
Button and/or snap (optional)

CUTTING

Cutting for Letter Pocket

From *each* of the reproduction prints, cut:
- 1 rectangle, 8" x 13" (2 total)

Cutting for Needle Case

From *each* of the reproduction prints, cut:
- 1 rectangle, 5" x 8½" (2 total)

ASSEMBLING THE LETTER POCKET

1. Layer the 8" x 13" lining rectangle with the 8" x 13" rectangle for the cover, right sides together. Place the 7¾" x 12¾" piece of interfacing on the top. Optional: to make rounded corners, use a small plate, bowl, or cup to draw a curve on each of the upper corners and trim the layers.

 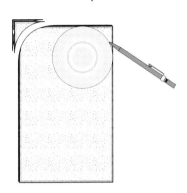

2. Using a ¼" seam, sew the layers together, catching the interfacing and leaving a 3" opening for turning. Trim the corners for smoother edges.

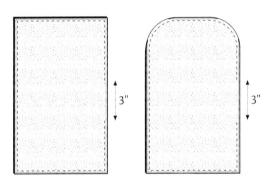

3. Turn the pocket right side out. Fold the seam allowances at the opening to the inside and press. Pin the opening closed. Fold the case approximately in thirds and pin the bottom part to form a pocket. Open the top flap and sew completely around the case, ¼" from the edge, beginning at one of the bottom edges. Remove the pins, fold the flap back down, and press the pocket well.

 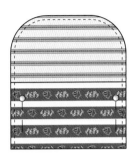

4. Sew a button onto the front of the flap, if desired, or sew a snap closure to the inside flap and pocket front.

ASSEMBLING THE NEEDLE CASE

Follow the steps for "Assembling the Letter Pocket" (at left) to put the needle case together; use the 5" x 8½" rectangle for the cover, the 5" x 8½" lining rectangle, and the 4¾" x 8¼" piece of interfacing. When the needle case is complete, insert the 2" x 3" piece of wool felt to hold the needles.

WITH THIS NEEDLE

From the kind hearts of the women,
Came the first of "Sewing-Circles,"
That the germ of all the others.
Lo! from that, a small beginning,
Farther, wider, spread the circles,
Till they covered all the region,
Till each village has its circles,
Every cause its Sewing-Circles.
For the Seamen some are sewing,
For the Heathen many others,
For the cause of Foreign Missions,

To advance the cause of Temperance,
To relieve the many sufferings,
All the countless woes and bitter,
Which that monster, Hydra-headed,
Intemperance, has created.
And a few are found among them,
Toiling for the cause of Freedom,
Toiling for the suffering slave;
Every movement philanthropic,
Finds among them many allies,
Many willing, helping sisters.

~Excerpt from: McElroy, E. P., The Sewing-Circles

Although the Women's Christian Temperance Union, one of the largest women's reform movements of the nineteenth century, was formed in 1874, temperance societies flourished in the United States earlier, during the middle part of the nineteenth century. Abraham Lincoln was a member of one and Susan B. Anthony, one of the leaders of the women's suffrage movement, joined the Daughters of Temperance in 1848.

Since women were not allowed to own property, were denied child custody, and had no legal recourse for abusive drunk husbands, many found themselves drawn to the Temperance movement, which set the stage for many to become involved in women's rights. Sometimes simplistically viewed today as a right wing, Christian organization intending to shut down saloons and stamp out alcohol, it was actually one of the first feminist movements and also the first national women's organization in the United States. The group focused on issues deemed important to women: child care for working women, support for rape victims, vocational training, better education, and the right to vote.

Hand sewing was a common part of life in the nineteenth century, and sewing circles and quilting bees flourished in rural towns across the nation. Once the war began, women were encouraged to sew items to be distributed through local aid societies or sold at fairs to raise money to support the troops. According to Pat Ferrero in *Hearts and Hands,* women's sewing also played a major role in their other reform activities, their needles used "as weapons in their campaigns against a variety of social ills and injustices." For instance, although women were involved in all aspects of the abolitionist movement before the war, the biggest role they played was in fundraising. Quilts and other needlework products were made and sold to raise money for a particular cause, first antislavery fairs and then sanitary fairs, organized by the U.S. Sanitary Commission, that spread across the nation.

The common attitude during this time and before the war was that a woman's "place" centered on the home. Women organized their sewing groups to support other important reform movements like tem-perance and suffrage as well. Sewing for these movements and other charity-related causes empowered women to effect social change "through their needle." Benevolent activities that many women were involved in were useful in helping them develop their skills and strengthen further community service work; this exposed these strengths, skills, and talents to the rest of the world in the years that followed, expanding women's opportunities and eventually leading to paid positions alongside men in varied professional roles.

Album Quilt

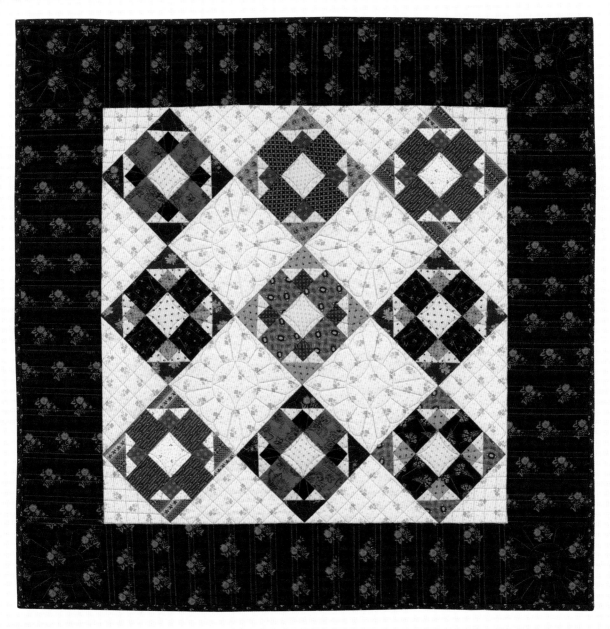

Machine quilted by Dawn Larsen.
Finished quilt: 36" x 36"
Finished block: 6" x 6"

Here's another great design to make for a friendship quilt project displaying the names of special people or perhaps favorite quotes or other sentiments, as they sometimes did in the nineteenth century with political statements. Personalize your album quilt by signing your name (or the names of others) in the light squares with a fine-point permanent marking pen.

MATERIALS

Yardage is based on 42"-wide, 100% cotton fabric.

¾ yard of red print for border

⅝ yard of light shirting print for setting blocks and triangles

⅝ yard *total* of assorted medium and dark prints for blocks

⅜ yard *total* of assorted light prints for blocks

⅜ yard of dark blue print for binding

1⅓ yards of fabric for backing

42" x 42" piece of cotton batting

CUTTING

Cutting for 1 Block (Cut 9 total.)

From one assorted light print, cut:

- 1 square, 2½" x 2½"
- 4 squares, 1⅞" x 1⅞"; cut in half diagonally to make 8 triangles

From one assorted medium or dark print, cut:

- 4 squares, 2½" x 2½"

From a second medium or dark print, cut:

- 2 squares, 2⅞" x 2⅞"; cut in half diagonally to make 4 triangles

From a third medium or dark print, cut:

- 4 squares, 1½" x 1½"

Cutting for the Remainder of the Quilt

From the light shirting print, cut:

- 4 squares, 6½" x 6½"
- 2 squares, 9¾" x 9¾"; cut into quarters diagonally to make 8 triangles
- 2 squares, 5⅛" x 5⅛"; cut in half diagonally to make 4 triangles

From the red print, cut:

- 2 strips, 5½" x 26"
- 2 strips, 5½" x 36"

From the dark blue print, cut:

- 4 strips, 2½" x 42"

MAKING THE BLOCKS

The directions are written for making one block at a time.

1. Sew two matching light print 1⅞" triangles to adjacent sides of a medium or dark 1½" square. Press the seam allowances toward the triangles. Make four.

Make 4.

2. Sew a medium or dark print 2⅞" triangle to the long edge of each unit from step 1. Press the seam allowances toward the larger triangles.

Make 4.

3. Arrange the units from step 2, four medium or dark print 2½" squares, and a light print 2½" square in rows as shown. Sew the rows and press the seam allowances toward the dark print squares. Sew the rows together to make the block.

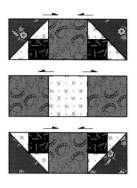 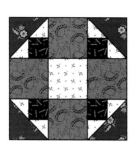

4. Repeat steps 1–3 to make a total of nine blocks.
5. If desired, follow the directions on page 41 for signing your Album blocks.

ASSEMBLING THE QUILT TOP

1. Referring to the quilt diagram, lay out the blocks, the light shirting 6½" squares, and the side setting triangles into diagonal rows. Sew the blocks into rows; press the seam allowances toward the setting pieces. Sew the rows together, pressing the seam allowances in opposite directions. Add the corner setting triangles and press toward the triangles.

2. Sew the red print 5½" x 26" strips to the sides of the quilt top. Press the seam allowances toward the border. Sew the red print 5½" x 36" strips to the top and bottom of the quilt. Press toward the border.

FINISHING THE QUILT

1. Layer the quilt top, batting, and backing; baste the layers together as shown in "Putting the Quilt Together" (page 75).
2. This quilt was machine quilted with a medallion design in the center of the blocks and straight lines in the border. Omit the quilting in the center of the blocks if you choose to add signatures.
3. Attach the binding to the quilt, referring to "Binding" (page 76).

Wool Appliqué Sewing Box

Wool appliqué by Katie Reed.

Finished appliqué: 3½" diameter

A sewing box was an important accessory for ladies in the nineteenth century. Their needles, thread, and buttons were kept inside, ready for embroidery work and sewing. Some boxes from this time period were works of art, made out of wood and often engraved and inlaid with brass or mother of pearl. Here's an easy appliqué project made with felted wool for the lid of a small box. Finish the box with acrylic paint from a craft store. It makes a great container for small pieces of jewelry too!

MATERIALS

4" x 4" square of black felted wool for appliqué foundation

Scraps of blue, red, gold, and green felted wool for appliqués

Pearl cotton, size 8, in black, gold, and green

Black button

4½" diameter round papier-mâché box*

Fusible web

Freezer paper

Glue**

Acrylic paint in light green and gray (or colors of your choice)

Small brush

*Available from craft stores

**Use permanent-bond fabric glue such as Aleene's OK To Wash-It.

MAKING THE APPLIQUÉ

1. Place the fusible web over the patterns for the flower, flower center, petals, and leaves (page 69) and trace the number of shapes needed, leaving about ½" of space between each. Trace the pattern for the background circle onto freezer paper. Cut out the pieces, leaving a scant ¼" or so around each piece.

2. Position the fusible web (for small pieces) and freezer paper (for background circle) on the wool pieces and press with a hot iron. Let cool. Cut out the shapes directly on the traced line and peel off the paper backing and freezer paper.

3. Arrange the gold flower and leaves on the black wool background circle, referring to the appliqué placement diagram at right. Press in place.

4. Using one strand of pearl cotton, sew a buttonhole stitch around the shapes. Use green pearl cotton around the small leaves and gold around the gold circle and the outer edge of the black circle.

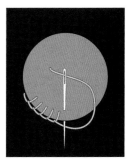

Buttonhole stitch

5. Position and press the blue flower petals to the design. Blanket-stitch using black pearl cotton. Add the red flower center and stitch with black pearl cotton.

6. Sew the button to the center.

Appliqué placement diagram

FINISHING THE BOX

1. Paint the box with acrylic paint, using several coats if necessary. I used pale green with a little bit of gray mixed in for an aged look. Let dry completely before placing the lid on top of the painted box. You can add a sealer or an antiquing glaze if desired.

2. Center the appliqué circle on top of the box and glue in place.

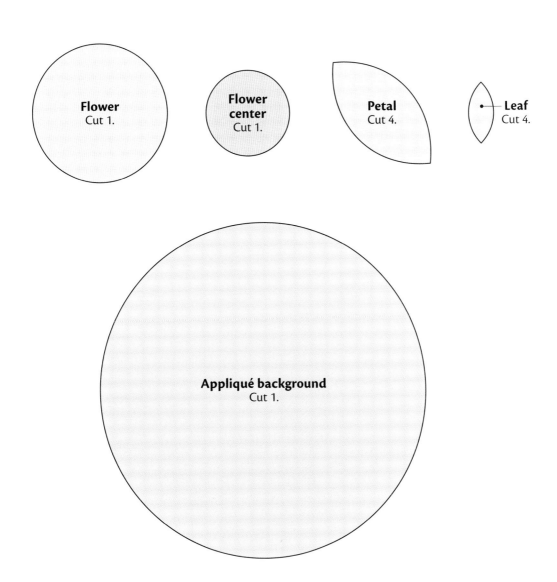

Flower
Cut 1.

Flower center
Cut 1.

Petal
Cut 4.

Leaf
Cut 4.

Appliqué background
Cut 1.

T Is for Temperance Quilt

Finished quilt: 19½" x 19½"
Finished block: 6" x 6"

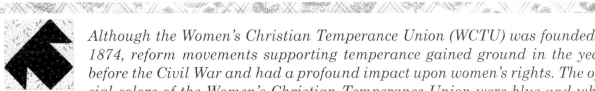

Although the Women's Christian Temperance Union (WCTU) was founded in 1874, reform movements supporting temperance gained ground in the years before the Civil War and had a profound impact upon women's rights. The official colors of the Women's Christian Temperance Union were blue and white and there was an abundance of quilts made in these colors toward the end of the nineteenth century.

MATERIALS

Yardage is based on 42"-wide, 100% cotton fabric.

¼ yard of medium blue print for outer border

1 fat eighth *each* of two different shirting prints for blocks

1 fat eighth *each* of two different blue prints for blocks

⅛ yard of dark blue print 1 for inner border

¼ yard of dark blue print 2 for binding

¾ yard of fabric for backing

24" x 24" piece of thin cotton batting

CUTTING

From *each* of the 2 shirting prints, cut:
- 1 square, 4⅞" x 4⅞" (2 total)
- 5 squares, 2⅞" x 2⅞" (10 total)

From *each* of the 2 blue prints for blocks, cut:
- 1 square, 4⅞" x 4⅞" (2 total)
- 5 squares, 2⅞" x 2⅞" (10 total)

From dark blue print 1, cut:
- 2 strips, 1½" x 12½"
- 2 strips, 1½" x 14½"

From the medium blue print for outer border, cut:
- 2 strips, 3" x 14½"
- 2 strips, 3" x 19½"

From dark blue print 2, cut:
- 3 strips, 1¼" x 42"

MAKING THE BLOCKS

You will make two pairs of identical blue-and-white T blocks. Pair up your fabrics before you begin to simplify the piecing.

1. Draw a diagonal line from corner to corner on the wrong side of each light 4⅞" square. Layer a marked square on top of a blue 4⅞" square, right sides together. Stitch ¼" from the line on both sides and cut on the drawn line. Press the seam allowances toward the darker fabric. Make four half-square-triangle units.

Make 4.

2. Draw a diagonal line on the wrong side of each light print 2⅞" square. Layer five matching light squares on top of five matching blue print 2⅞" squares, right sides together. Stitch ¼" from the line on both sides and cut on the drawn line. Press the seam allowances toward the darker fabric. Make 20 half-square-triangle units in matching sets of 10.

Make 20.

3. Arrange the matching units from steps 1 and 2 as shown; sew the block together in sections. Sew the sections together and press. Make four blocks.

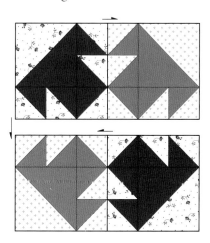

Make 4.

ASSEMBLING THE QUILT TOP

1. Sew the blocks together as shown.

2. Sew the dark blue 1½" x 12½" strips to the sides of the quilt top, pressing the seam allowances toward the border. Sew the dark blue 1½" x 14½" strips to the top and bottom of the quilt and press.

3. Sew the medium blue 3" x 14½" strips to the top and bottom of the quilt top, pressing the seam allowances toward the outer border. Sew the medium blue 3" x 19½" strips to the sides of the quilt top and press.

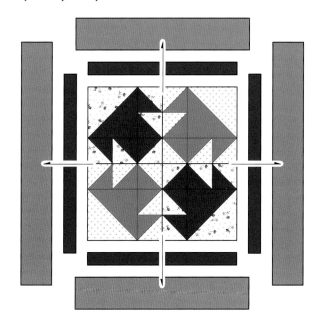

FINISHING THE QUILT

1. Layer the quilt top, batting, and backing; baste the layers together as shown in "Putting the Quilt Together" (page 75).

2. The quilt shown was hand quilted in the ditch and with a T motif in the corner triangles.

3. Attach binding to the quilt, referring to "Single-Fold Binding" (page 77).

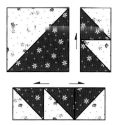

QUILTMAKING BASICS

If you look at antique quilts from the nineteenth century, you'll notice that many of the ones that we treasure today aren't perfect by any means. Women of the time did not have all of the tools, accessories, or techniques that are available to quilters today. Nor did they have the wide variety of quilting books that we have for inspiration. This didn't keep them from quilting, however, and they learned and improved their skills as they made their amazing quilts. Keep this in mind if you're a beginner; don't worry about perfection as you embark on your quiltmaking journey. That will come with experience.

For most of the quilts in this book, all you need are basic sewing skills and a machine in good working order. Use a ¼" seam allowance and try to be accurate. If your machine does not have a ¼" foot, place a strip of masking tape on the throat plate exactly ¼" from the needle and use this as a guide as you are sewing.

BASIC TOOLS

These are the tools you'll need to make the quilts in the book.

- **Rotary cutter.** A medium-sized cutter (45 mm) will enable you to cut strips and trim small pieces.
- **Rotary-cutting mat.** Use this gridded surface for cutting fabric. An 18" x 24" mat is a good choice.
- **Ruler.** Use a clear plastic ruler that's at least 4" x 12" and designed to be used with a rotary cutter. The measurements should be clearly marked. A 6" square ruler also comes in handy for squaring up your blocks. A 4" square ruler is helpful for making half-square-triangle units.
- **Pins.** Use sharp pins to hold your pieces while sewing. Small appliqué pins will keep small pieces from shifting.
- **Thread.** Always use 100% cotton thread for your piecing; use quilting thread, which is coated, for hand quilting.
- **Needles.** Use 80/12 sewing-machine needles for machine piecing. Change your needle after every major project to be sure your needle is always

sharp. You will need basic hand-sewing needles for sewing bindings, needles called Sharps for appliqué, and needles called Betweens for hand quilting.
- **Seam ripper.** Expect to make some mistakes but don't worry too much about them. If you do make a mistake, a seam ripper will help you easily remove the stitches to correct it.
- **Iron and pressing surface.** Any iron with a cotton setting will work for pressing your quilt pieces. You'll need a flat surface for pressing, such as an ironing board or pressing mat.

A Note about Fabrics

Many of you may feel the same as I do—that reproduction fabrics impart a real sense of history in traditional quilts. I use quite a lot of fabrics modeled after prints that were popular during the nineteenth century. But, when making the quilts, please don't let yourself be limited by my choices—if you prefer to use contemporary prints in your projects, they'll turn out great. The nice thing about traditional quilt patterns is that they are time-tested. They've been around for a very long time, and are still being used today in modern-day quilting that uses contemporary fabrics as well as reproduction fabrics.

ROTARY CUTTING

Accurate cutting is an important part of making any quilt, large or small. If your pieces are not cut properly, the piecing may be difficult and the quilt measurements will be off. Cutting is also important for conserving your fabric, although with many of these quilts, because they use a variety of scraps, more than enough yardage is given in the pattern directions.

While strip piecing and cutting don't generally work well with scrap quilts, since no two blocks are exactly the same, you *can* layer your fabrics and cut multiple pieces at the same time.

MAKING HALF-SQUARE-TRIANGLE UNITS

Many of the quilts in this book use a simple technique for making half-square-triangle units.

1. Cut the squares to the size designated in the pattern. Pair up two of the squares, a lighter square and a darker square, according to the directions.
2. Draw a diagonal line from corner to corner on the wrong side of the lighter square.
3. Layer the marked square on top of the other square, right sides together. Stitch ¼" away from the line on both sides. Cut on the drawn line to make two half-square-triangle units. Press the seam allowances toward the darker fabric, being careful not to stretch the pieces. Trim the dog-ear pieces at the corners.

Troubleshooting Triangle Units
If your half-square-triangle units turn out slightly smaller than they should, mark the stitching lines as well as the line that goes from corner to corner. Mark and sew a scant ¼" away from the center diagonal line. Since many of the half-square-triangle units I make for my quilts are small, I keep a 4" square ruler near my cutting mat when I'm trimming the units and use it to make sure they are square and the correct size.

PRESSING

Always press each seam after sewing. Press the seam allowances to one side, toward the darker fabric, if possible. When joining pieces, blocks, or rows of blocks, press the seam allowances in opposite directions to make lining up the seams (when sewing) less difficult. Pressing in this way will allow the seams to line up more easily and the blocks will go together correctly.

Opposing seams

SQUARING UP YOUR BLOCKS

Squaring up your blocks will ensure that the pieces of your quilt, the sashing, and the borders will fit together nicely. Before you piece your blocks together, check to see that they are the same size. Uneven blocks are usually caused by incorrectly sewing the seam allowances. Sometimes all that's needed is to redo a seam that is too small or too large. Also, check your pressing. Incorrect pressing can cause distortion in the pieces. If you use a steam iron, like I prefer to, make sure that you press carefully without stretching the fabric or your pieces will definitely become distorted.

Find the center of your block and place a clear square ruler (a 6" square is a good choice) on top, using the grid lines to line up the pieces in the block and trim if they are uneven.

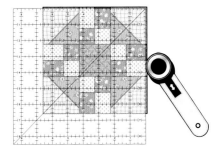

BORDERS

The border will do much to enhance the quilt if it's chosen well. Select the fabric for the borders after the quilt top is completed. Make sure the print in the fabric isn't so busy that it detracts from the quilt. A good rule of thumb is, if the main part of the quilt is very busy with many scrappy pieces, try to tone it down with a "quiet" border; choose a fabric that has a low contrast rather than a large print. The border should frame the quilt, not take over. Lively borders work best when the rest of the quilt has a subdued tone and contains plain blocks or blocks with few contrasting pieces.

It's important to measure the sewn quilt top before cutting the border strips, especially on large quilts, since slight piecing variations can affect the measurements. Measure the center in both directions and cut the borders as directed.

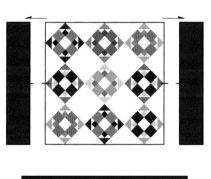

PUTTING THE QUILT TOGETHER

Square up the four corners of your quilt top using a square ruler. Trim the four sides, if necessary, by lining up your long ruler from one corner to the opposite corner and trimming away any excess fabric.

Some of the larger quilts in the book were made with pieced backings. Sew the pieces together with a ¼" seam allowance in one of the three ways shown

below. Cut the backing at least 3" larger in length *and* width than the quilt top.

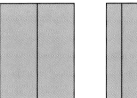

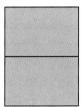

Use a thin, low-loft cotton batting for the soft, flat look seen in many antique quilts. Cut the batting at least 3" larger in length and width than the quilt top. Lay the backing on a clean, level surface. Smooth out any wrinkles and use masking tape to secure the corners. Layer the batting and quilt top over the backing. Use thread for hand quilting or safety pins for machine quilting to baste the layers together.

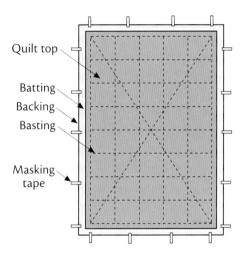

QUILTING

Many quilts made in the nineteenth century were utilitarian and featured simple quilting designs like straight-line quilting or in-the-ditch quilting. I enjoyed quilting some of the smaller quilts in this book by hand and I recommend it if you have the time. While it may seem time consuming to hand quilt your quilts, it's a perfect way to give your quilt that special handmade touch. If you're hesitant to try, begin by using a simple quilting design on one of the doll quilts. With a little practice you'll get better and I predict you'll enjoy the handwork.

Cut an 18" length of neutral-colored quilting thread or a thread color that matches the fabrics in the quilt top. You can use a contrasting color of thread if you want your stitches to stand out. Try to keep your stitches even; however, sometimes a little irregularity in the stitches adds to the charm of the quilt. Remember, most antique quilts weren't perfect by any means, and part of their charm is in the handmade look.

Simply Quilted

Hand quilting a small quilt can be very relaxing. If you're a beginner and hesitant to quilt by hand, try quilting simple straight lines at first. Take advantage of tools that make quilting easier, such as quilting stencils and water-soluble marking pens to mark quilting lines. There's also a special tape called Tiger Tape that's marked with lines to help you learn to space your stitches evenly. Quilting on small quilts really doesn't have to be perfect—you'll get better with practice. Or maybe, like me, you'll find that it doesn't matter if your stitches aren't perfect. They'll have the naive charm we love so much in the antique doll quilts.

BINDING

To prepare the quilt for binding, use your ruler and rotary cutter to straighten the edges of the quilt and make sure the corners form right angles. Trim away any excess batting and backing. Cut the number of strips from binding fabric in the required width as instructed in the project instructions. There should be enough length to go around your quilt plus 10" extra for mitering corners and joining strips. For large quilts, use a double-fold binding with strips cut 2½" wide. For small, doll-sized quilts, use a single-fold binding with strips cut 1¼" wide.

Double-Fold Binding

1. Join the strips using a diagonal seam and press the seam allowances open. Fold the strips in half, wrong sides together, and press.

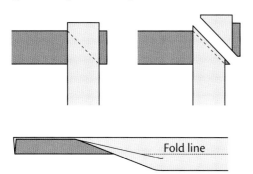

2. Position the binding along one side of the quilt top, aligning the raw edges.

3. Leaving a 5" piece of binding free, begin stitching the binding to the quilt top, starting at the center of one side and using a ¼" seam allowance. Sew through all of the layers. A walking foot is helpful to feed the layers through evenly when attaching binding. Stop sewing ¼" from the first corner and backstitch.

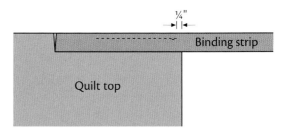

4. Remove the quilt from the machine. Turn the quilt and fold the binding straight up, making a 45° angle. Fold the binding back down, aligning it with the edge of the next side. Continue sewing the remaining sides in this way.

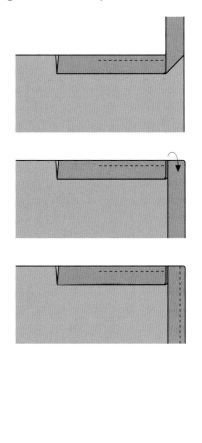

5. Stop stitching about 5" from where you started and remove the quilt from the machine. Overlap the beginning and ending pieces of binding and trim so that the overlap equals the width that you cut your binding strips.

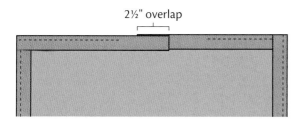

2½" overlap

6. Unfold the strips and place them right sides together at a right angle. Sew on the diagonal and trim away the excess fabric. Place the binding back over the quilt and finish sewing it in place.

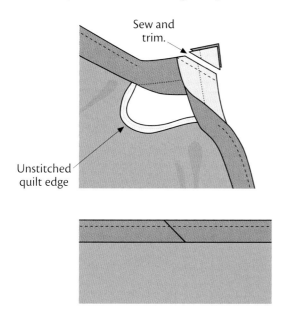

Sew and trim.

Unstitched quilt edge

7. Turn the binding over to the back of the quilt and stitch it to the quilt with a blind stitch using matching thread. Miter the corners as shown.

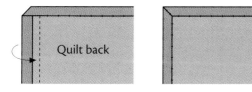

Quilt back

Single-Fold Binding

I like to use a single-fold binding on my small quilts because it adds less bulk, and a double-fold binding is not needed for durability.

1. Follow steps 1–6 for "Double-Fold Binding," but use strips that are cut 1¼" wide. *Do not* press the binding strips in half with right sides together.

2. Turn the binding over to the back of the quilt. Turn the raw edge under ¼" and slip-stitch it to the back of the quilt using matching thread. Miter each of the corners as shown.

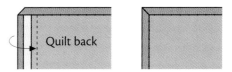

Quilt back

LABEL YOUR QUILTS

We may not think much about it when we're making our quilts, but we're leaving behind a legacy every time we take a stitch. Don't you wish quilters from the past had listed their names and dates or other information on the back of their quilts? Family members and future generations may thank you someday for taking the time to add a label to your quilt.

It's easy to make a simple label by ironing a piece of double-sided fusible web (for stability when writing) to a neutral piece of fabric or a small piece of muslin. At the very least, sign your name and the date using a fine-tip permanent marker. If the quilt was made for a special occasion, add a little information about that to preserve the memory. Fuse the label to the back of the quilt. Hand stitch ⅛" along the edge with a simple running stitch in a contrasting-colored thread, making sure you don't stitch through to the front of the quilt.

Another idea is to appliqué a leftover block from the front of the quilt to the back and sign your name and the date.

Kathleen Tracy
2010

BIBLIOGRAPHY

Ferrero, Pat, Elaine Hedges, and Julie Silber. *Hearts and Hands: The Influence of Women and Quilts on American Society.* San Francisco: Quilt Digest Press, 1987.

Flexner, Eleanor. *Century of Struggle: The Woman's Rights Movement in the United States.* New York: Atheneum, 1968.

Fox, Sandi. *For Purpose and Pleasure: Quilting Together in Nineteenth-Century America.* Nashville: Rutledge Hill Press, 1995.

Hackett, Horatio B. *Christian Memorials of the War: Or, Scenes and Incidents Illustrative of Religious Faith and Principle, Patriotism and Bravery in Our Army.* Boston: Gould and Lincoln, 1864.

Jackson, Donald Dale. *Twenty Million Yankees: The Northern Home Front.* Alexandria, VA: Time-Life Books, 1985.

Kiracofe, Roderick with Mary Elizabeth Johnson. *The American Quilt: A History of Cloth and Comfort 1750–1950.* New York: Clarkson Potter, 1993.

Leonard, Elizabeth D. *Yankee Women: Gender Battles in the Civil War.* New York: W. W. Norton & Co., 1994.

McElroy, E. P. *The Sewing-Circles: A composition read before the Bowdoin Literary Association, of Dorchester, at their annual exhibition, Tuesday evening, March 25, 1856.* Boston: William White, 1856.

Moore, Frank. *Women of the War: True Stories of Brave Women in the Civil War.* New York: Blue/Grey Books, 1997.

Pickett, George E. *The Heart of a Soldier: As Revealed in the Intimate Letters of General George E. Pickett.* New York: S. Moyle, 1913.

Silber, Nina. *Daughters of the Union: Northern Women Fight the Civil War.* Cambridge, MA: Harvard University Press, 2005.

Spicer, William Arnold. *History of the Ninth and Tenth Regiments Rhode Island Volunteers.* Providence, RI: Snow & Franham, 1892. Digitized by the New York Public Library.

Sutherland, Daniel E. *The Expansion of Everyday Life 1860–1876.* New York: Harper & Row, 1989.

ABOUT THE AUTHOR

Kathleen Tracy has been playing with fabric and has been fascinated with color since childhood. Designing quilts became a great way of expressing that creative impulse. After working in the publishing industry for many years, learning to quilt by making quilts for her daughter's American Girl dolls led to a career writing quilt-pattern books. Kathleen is best known for books that combine a little bit of history with quilts that use traditional patterns from the past. She is also the author of *American Doll Quilts* (Martingale & Company, 2004), *Prairie Children and Their Quilts* (Martingale & Company, 2006), and *Remembering Adelia* (Martingale & Company, 2009). When she's not quilting, she can be found reading, writing, or walking dogs! Kathleen lives in Deerfield, Illinois, with her husband, two children, and two dogs.

There's More Online!
Visit Kathy at www.countrylanequilts.com and read her blog at http://sentimentalquilter.blogspot.com. Find other great books on quilts and crafts at www.martingale-pub.com.

You might also enjoy these other fine titles from

MARTINGALE & COMPANY

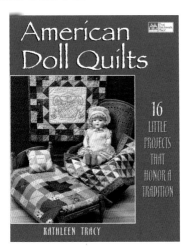

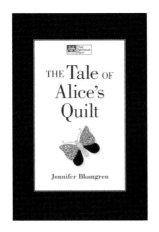

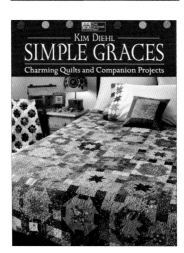